READER'S DIGEST

ANIMAL
INSTINCTS

A DAY AT THE WATERHOLE

Over 24 hours, an African waterhole is a showcase for a wide variety of instinct-driven behaviour, as animals arrive at different times to drink, while local residents go about their daily activities. Waterholes can be dangerous places for some creatures, as predators often wait around for prey animals to appear.

▶ DEADLY DUEL

As the Sun climbs high overhead, a crocodile seizes its chance to grab a wildebeest that has come to drink. In the crocodile, instinct has produced the ultimate sit-and-wait predator, lying unseen in the shallows. When a victim comes within range, it bursts out of the water – often with lethal results.

▶ SHADY BUSINESS

Black herons instinctively spread their wings as they wade, luring fish that like to hide in shade.

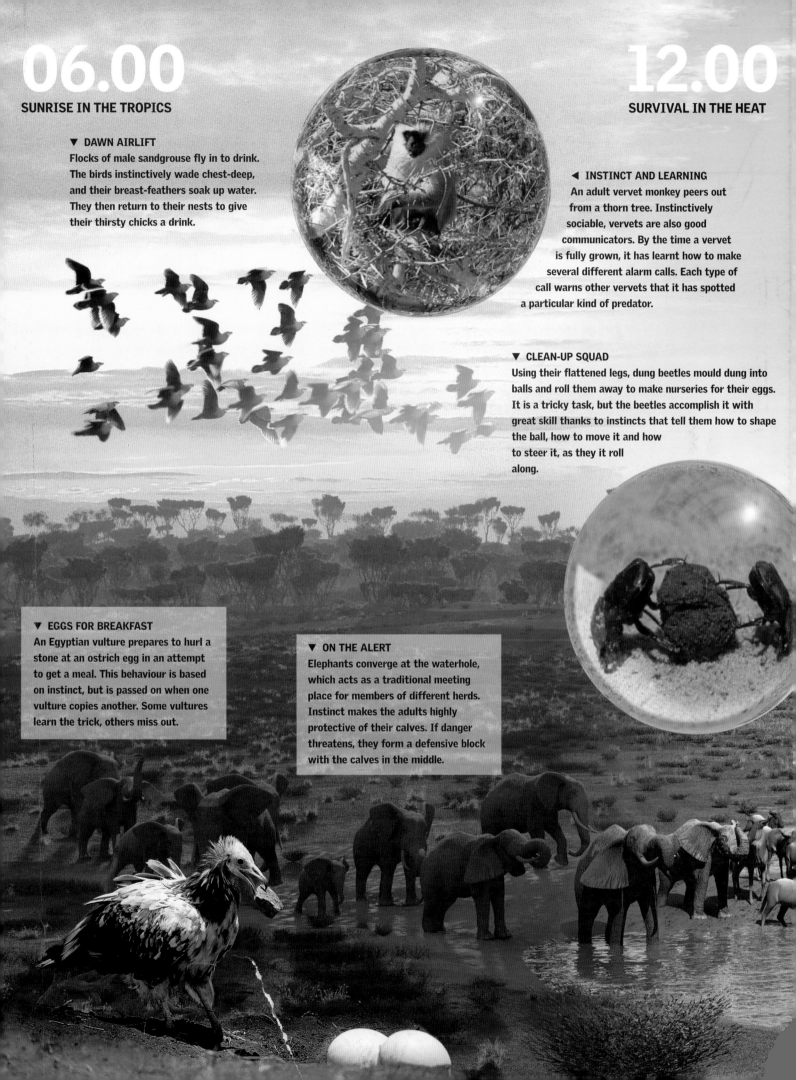

06.00
SUNRISE IN THE TROPICS

12.00
SURVIVAL IN THE HEAT

▼ **DAWN AIRLIFT**
Flocks of male sandgrouse fly in to drink. The birds instinctively wade chest-deep, and their breast-feathers soak up water. They then return to their nests to give their thirsty chicks a drink.

◄ **INSTINCT AND LEARNING**
An adult vervet monkey peers out from a thorn tree. Instinctively sociable, vervets are also good communicators. By the time a vervet is fully grown, it has learnt how to make several different alarm calls. Each type of call warns other vervets that it has spotted a particular kind of predator.

▼ **CLEAN-UP SQUAD**
Using their flattened legs, dung beetles mould dung into balls and roll them away to make nurseries for their eggs. It is a tricky task, but the beetles accomplish it with great skill thanks to instincts that tell them how to shape the ball, how to move it and how to steer it, as they it roll along.

▼ **EGGS FOR BREAKFAST**
An Egyptian vulture prepares to hurl a stone at an ostrich egg in an attempt to get a meal. This behaviour is based on instinct, but is passed on when one vulture copies another. Some vultures learn the trick, others miss out.

▼ **ON THE ALERT**
Elephants converge at the waterhole, which acts as a traditional meeting place for members of different herds. Instinct makes the adults highly protective of their calves. If danger threatens, they form a defensive block with the calves in the middle.

INSTINCT CONTROLS ANIMAL WORLD. VERY START OF LIFE, TO CARRY OUT COMPLEX THE NEED TO LEARN. HABITATS, FROM OCEAN DEPTHS, THIS GIVES ANIMALS THE SUCCESS IN THEIR

BEHAVIOUR IN THE INBUILT FROM THE IT ENABLES ANIMALS BEHAVIOUR WITHOUT IN ALL THE WORLD'S DESERTS TO THE MYSTERIOUS FORCE BEST CHANCE OF STRUGGLE TO SURVIVE.

▼ PRIVATE LARDER

Gripping with claws and teeth, an adult leopard drags a carcass into a tree. This instinct has a very practical value, because it keeps the remains away from scavengers, such as hyenas. Unlike lions, leopards are solitary hunters. They wait until darkness falls before setting off.

► MATING DANCE

In the heat of the night, two scorpions carry out an elaborate mating dance. Instinct calls the steps as they grip each other by the pincers, which keeps each of them beyond the reach of the other's sting. The male places a package of sperm on the ground, and manoeuvres the female into position so that her reproductive system picks it up.

▲ NIGHT FLIGHT

A bent-wing bat swoops down over the waterhole to catch moths and other flying insects. Most bats emerge soon after sunset, but their feeding behaviour varies according to species. Most insect-eating species catch their prey in midair, but some snatch it from leaves and bushes, or even from the ground. Other species specialise in catching frogs, and a few live on fish, homing in on the ripples they make – even in total darkness.

◄ OVERNIGHT STOP

Flocks of barn swallows arrive to roost among reeds at the water's edge. These swallows breed in Europe and Asia, but every autumn instinct sends them south to spend the winter in warmer climes. While there, their breeding instincts shut down and they concentrate on feeding.

▼ CAUTIOUS APPROACH

Like all potential prey, giraffe are instinctively cautious. They are also in a particularly vulnerable position when drinking, with head down and front legs spread, so one drinks while the others keep watch.

▼ TEAMWORK

A pride of lions goes hunting. In lion this involves a complex combinatic of instinct and learning. Instinct drives their overall strategy, which is based on stealth and surprise. Learning improves their teamwork

◄ CAREFUL PARENTS

A male giant waterbug carries a batch of eggs that the female, prompted by instinct, has glued to his back. Once the eggs are in place, he can no longer fly. His behaviour is a rare example of parental care in insects, as most species leave their eggs to hatch on their own.

ANIMAL
INSTINCTS

1 LIVING BY INSTINCT

18 DOING WHAT COMES NATURALLY
22 BEHAVIOUR THAT ADDS UP
26 TRIGGERED INTO ACTION
30 INSTINCTS AND LEARNING
32 CULTURE CLUB

2 RHYTHMS OF LIFE

36 KEEPING IN STEP
42 TIMETABLES OF LIFE

5 FINDING FOOD

92 THE HUNT FOR FOOD
98 ESCAPE ARTISTS
100 SCAVENGERS
102 PLANT EATERS
106 NATURAL MEDICINES
109 USING TOOLS

6 MEETING

114 ANIMAL ENCOUNTERS
118 KNOWING YOUR PLACE
120 MAKING UP
122 INNER CONFLICT
124 HOW BEHAVIOUR EVOLVES

3 THE MATING IMPERATIVE

52 INSTINCT VERSUS INSTINCT
54 FINDING A MATE
62 COURTSHIP RITUALS
66 TESTS OF STRENGTH
68 MATING

4 STARTING OUT

72 APPROACHES TO PARENTING
78 CANNIBALISM
80 FAMILY TIES
82 FEEDING
84 DEFENDING THE YOUNG
88 GROWING UP

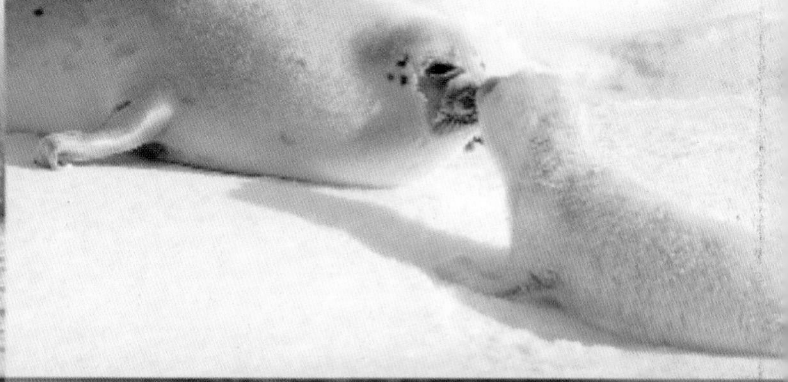

7 ANIMAL LANGUAGE

128 COMMUNICATE
136 TALKING TO US

8 FINDING THE WAY

140 ANIMALS AT HOME
148 MIGRATION

INTRODUCTION

THROUGHOUT THE ANIMAL KINGDOM, INSTINCT IS CONSTANTLY AT WORK, TRIGGERING INHERITED PATTERNS OF BEHAVIOUR THAT HELP EVERY CREATURE TO SURVIVE. Instinct operates in all animals, wherever and however they live. And it makes itself felt across a broad scale of activities. At one extreme, it lies behind the precise movements that a fly uses to clean it wings, or those that a young bird makes when it chips its way out of an egg. At the other extreme, it triggers and oversees some of Nature's greatest spectacles, such as the courtship dances of cranes, or the mass migration of wildebeest across East Africa's open plains.

Human behaviour depends mainly on learning and insight, which makes it difficult for us to imagine the **tremendous power** that instinct exerts in the lives of animals. When birds migrate, or beavers build their dams, when honeybees swarm or termites make their nests, they all seem to know what they are doing, but nothing could be further from the truth. As far as we know, very few animals are capable of abstract reasoning or planning ahead. Instead, **instinct controls them**, rather like a computer program, making them react to conditions and events around them in predictable ways. Bird migration

provides stunning proof of this. Some young birds, such as Eurasian cuckoos, travel thousands of miles, to places they have never seen before, entirely on their own. Thanks to their inherited 'software', they do not need an adult bird to show them the way.

This **inherited know-how** reveals itself in many other **extraordinary skills**. It guides cleaner fish as they tidy up their clients, and spiders as they spin their webs. And it enables animals of all kinds to **carry out the essential tasks** of everyday life: to communicate, locate food and water, hunt, defend themselves and their young, find a mate and raise young. It also allows animals to **fit in with nature's rhythms**, often preparing them for changes weeks or even months before they actually occur.

Early naturalists struggled to explain how animals managed to carry out these feats. It was only in the early 20th century that scientists began to look at instincts and behaviour in a methodical way. Their work revealed a fascinating spectrum between **instinctive behaviour**, which is passed on intact when animals breed, and **learned behaviour**, which is gradually built up during an animal's lifetime. We lie at one end of this spectrum, because most of our behaviour is learned. At the other extreme, simple animals, such as flatworms and sea slugs, live in a world that is dominated by instinct, and where learning plays only a minor role. Between these extremes lies a huge array of animals, from fish and octopuses to cats and dogs, whose lives are governed partly by instinct, and partly by learning and experience.

Unlike learned behaviour, instinct has been at work since animal life began, over 1 billion years ago. Because it is inherited, it **evolves** – just as animal species do. This is its most powerful feature, because over countless generations, it becomes finely honed to **fit an animal's needs**. Some of the most important instincts – such as the urge to breed – are found throughout the animal world, even though they **differ from one species to another**. But many, such as the ones that control migration, are highly developed in some animals but completely absent in others. Instincts can also **evolve different uses** as time goes by. When a fly cleans its wings, it is keeping in trim for flight. But when one bird preens another, it sends out a message, defusing tension or cementing a close bond. Thanks to adaptations like this,

each animal inherits **a behavioural package** that deals with all the demands, dangers and opportunities of everyday life.

Today, scientists know more than ever before about the way instincts work. Research has shown how they are triggered into action, and how they are passed on from one generation to another. Fascinating insights also come from occasions when **instinct backfires** – for example, when a bird attacks its own reflection or a moth spirals into a flame. But we still have a vast amount to learn. Instinct runs deep, and its hidden influence helps to make the living world work.

ON THE MOVE
A herd of elephants makes its way across the Kenyan savannah towards a waterhole. Elephants travel a long way to find food and water, and use ancient routes to do so. This urge to migrate is dictated by instinct, but the routes have to be learnt.

LIVING
INSTI

BY NCT 1

GRIPPING A BRANCH IN ITS TEETH, A BEAVER MOVES THROUGH THE WATER TO PUT THE FINISHING TOUCHES TO A DAM. Beavers know nothing about physics, hydraulics or engineering, or even why water flows downhill. Even so, the dams they make are among nature's greatest constructions. They are capable of holding back thousands, even millions of gallons of water, and they can last for over a century, even though they are built with nothing more than branches, sticks and mud. How do beavers do it? Through patterns of behaviour – or instincts – that they inherit from their parents and which are hard-wired into their brains. Beavers do not need to learn about dam-building, although practice improves their expertise. Instead, they already have the skills they need, waiting to be used, even before they are born.

DOING WHAT COMES
NATURALLY

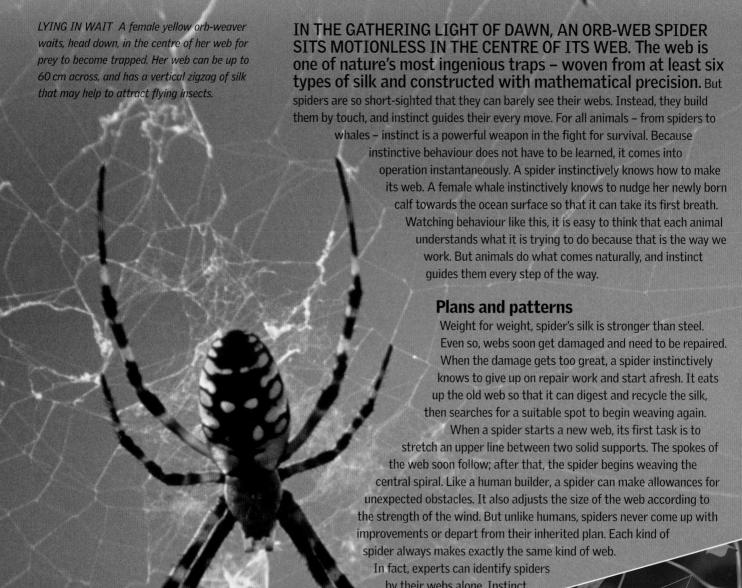

LYING IN WAIT A female yellow orb-weaver waits, head down, in the centre of her web for prey to become trapped. Her web can be up to 60 cm across, and has a vertical zigzag of silk that may help to attract flying insects.

IN THE GATHERING LIGHT OF DAWN, AN ORB-WEB SPIDER SITS MOTIONLESS IN THE CENTRE OF ITS WEB. The web is one of nature's most ingenious traps – woven from at least six types of silk and constructed with mathematical precision. But spiders are so short-sighted that they can barely see their webs. Instead, they build them by touch, and instinct guides their every move. For all animals – from spiders to whales – instinct is a powerful weapon in the fight for survival. Because instinctive behaviour does not have to be learned, it comes into operation instantaneously. A spider instinctively knows how to make its web. A female whale instinctively knows to nudge her newly born calf towards the ocean surface so that it can take its first breath. Watching behaviour like this, it is easy to think that each animal understands what it is trying to do because that is the way we work. But animals do what comes naturally, and instinct guides them every step of the way.

Plans and patterns

Weight for weight, spider's silk is stronger than steel. Even so, webs soon get damaged and need to be repaired. When the damage gets too great, a spider instinctively knows to give up on repair work and start afresh. It eats up the old web so that it can digest and recycle the silk, then searches for a suitable spot to begin weaving again. When a spider starts a new web, its first task is to stretch an upper line between two solid supports. The spokes of the web soon follow; after that, the spider begins weaving the central spiral. Like a human builder, a spider can make allowances for unexpected obstacles. It also adjusts the size of the web according to the strength of the wind. But unlike humans, spiders never come up with improvements or depart from their inherited plan. Each kind of spider always makes exactly the same kind of web. In fact, experts can identify spiders by their webs alone. Instinct is efficient, reliable and, above all, predictable.

THE WAITING GAME

Animals that work largely by instinct can spend days, months or even years waiting for something to happen, and when it does, they instinctively spring into action. Female ticks, which feed by sucking blood from mammals, are among the most patient players of this waiting game. They hatch on the ground, but have an instinct to climb up grasses and other soft-stemmed plants – putting them in the right place to jump aboard their hosts. Once a tick reaches the tip of a grassblade, it waits with its front legs outstretched, and can stay like this for months. Ticks cannot see animals from a distance, but they can sense movement and detect chemicals in breath and sweat. As an animal approaches, the tick's instincts put it on action stations. It waits until its own grassblade trembles, then launches itself at its target and scrambles aboard.

A question of timing

For spiders, weaving a web is a routine operation, like eating a meal. But some instincts control once-in-a-lifetime events that are vital for an animal's survival. For birds, one of these takes place at the very start of life, when a chick pecks its way out of its egg.

For a baby bird, hatching is a hazardous process. It can expect little or no help from its parents, but it has two pieces of equipment to help with the task: a sharp point, called an egg-tooth, at the tip of the beak, and a set of well-developed muscles on the sides of the neck and head. The chick uses these muscles to tap its egg-tooth against the inside of the shell. Every time it breaks through, it instinctively twists its body inside the shell and starts tapping again. Eventually, when the chick has turned full circle, it gives a powerful push with its legs. If all goes well, the blunt end of the shell breaks open like a lid, and the chick tumbles out of the shell and into the nest.

Hatching behaviour follows a strict timetable, but many instincts do not work like that. Instead of cutting in at a preset time, they are triggered by external events that can occur at any time. Many animals, on sensing something dark moving into view, instinctively dash for cover. This escape instinct makes good sense because the shadow could be a predator, and a split-second delay might have fatal results. For plant-eaters particularly, escape behaviour is a crucial part of survival.

SPINNING A WEB An orb-web spider starts its web by stretching a strand of silk between two supports, and hanging from it the first three spokes of the wheel. It then adds more spokes and the web's outer rim. Next, it weaves a temporary spiral, working out from the centre. Finally, it works its way back in, eating up the temporary spiral and replacing it with a permanent spiral of sticky silk.

BASIC INSTINCTS

WHEN A BIRD GLIDES ABOVE A CLIFFTOP OR A TIGER STALKS ITS PREY, DOZENS OF SEPARATE PIECES OF BEHAVIOUR ARE AT WORK AT THE SAME TIME. Some of these are purely instinctive, while others have to be learned. Many more kinds of behaviour are a subtle mixture of the two. These blurred boundaries make the study of pure instinct more difficult than it sounds, and to see it at work, scientists often turn to creatures that are so simple they have no brains or nervous systems at all.

One such creature is paramecium, a microscopic speck of living matter that thrives in pools and ponds. Paramecium consists of a single cell covered in hairlike filaments and it moves by beating its thousands of tiny hairs, which work like miniature oars. If it hits an obstacle as it travels through the water, it obeys a simple rule: it reverses, turns slightly and speeds forwards again, like a fairground dodgem car.

Paramecium relies on this inbuilt programme to navigate around its watery world. But where is this instinct housed in something that has no brain? The answer is that it is an inbuilt part of paramecium's chemistry – the part that controls the movement of its 'oars'. Scientists have been able to confirm this through the discovery of a mutant strain of paramecium that can swim forwards, but not backwards. In these, the 'dodgem' instinct cannot work, leaving the hapless mutants nudging endlessly at anything in their way.

> All features of an animal's body, including nerves and hormones, are controlled by genes. As a result, instinct is also controlled by genes – a set of instructions present in every cell.

Emergency action

Unlike paramecium, simple animals have nervous systems, although they have no brains. Sea anemones and jellyfish, for example, have a network of nerve cells extending throughout their bodies. Despite having less than a billionth of the number of nerve cells that we do, this is still enough to trigger instinctive movements that play a vital part in their survival. One of these is the withdrawal reflex – a movement shared by almost every animal in the living world, including ourselves.

The withdrawal reflex is a potential lifesaver, whether or not an animal happens to have a brain. It comes into action the moment any part of the body senses something that could be dangerous, such as heat or pain. Within a split second, nerves flash signals to muscles, which pull the affected bodypart away.

Unlike sea anemones or jellyfish, we can consciously choose to override the reflex, but when our attention is elsewhere it stays on guard, and has absolute control.

Instinctive behaviour can also be activated by chemical messengers, or hormones, which are released into an animal's blood. Each hormone targets a range of cells in the body, altering the way they work. Adrenaline is a hormone that prepares animals for 'fight or flight' when danger strikes. It speeds up an animal's heartbeat, deepens its breathing and releases reserves of glucose so that muscles have the energy they need to work unusually hard. Adrenaline acts in seconds, but other hormones take longer, such as those that trigger the complex behaviour needed to court a mate or raise a family.

Musical families

All features of an animal's body, including nerves and hormones, are controlled by genes. As a result, instinct is also controlled by genes – a set of instructions present in every cell, passed on by parents when they breed. Genes direct all kinds of instinctive behaviour, from the routes that animals take when they migrate to the way houseflies groom their wings.

In nature, species usually keep their genes to themselves. They do this by breeding only with their own kind. But in the laboratory, closely related species can sometimes be persuaded to interbreed – something that throws a fascinating light on the way that instinct is passed on. One such experiment involved two species of field cricket that are found in Australia. In both species, the males have a characteristic song, which they make by scraping their wings together. When the two species were encouraged to interbreed, all the young crickets produced the same song – but one that was different from the songs made by their parents. This new song was scripted entirely by instinct from the moment the young crickets warmed up to make their first chirp.

Geese on guard

Rather than inheriting all of their behaviour in their genes, vertebrates learn much of what they do, but they

PARENTS ON DUTY While its mate keeps guard, a Canada goose carefully turns her eggs to make sure that they are equally warmed all over. If an egg accidentally falls out of the nest, the parent goose instinctively knows how to roll it back.

still show examples of purely instinctive behaviour as well. To identify behaviour in vertebrates that is purely instinctive, scientists look for a telltale sign: unlike learned behaviour, pure instinct is stereotyped – once it starts, it always works in the same, predictable way.

During the 1930s, one of the pioneers of research into animal behaviour, the Austrian zoologist Konrad Lorenz, began studying behaviour in geese. He discovered, among other things, that an instinctive response is triggered in nesting geese if one of their eggs accidentally rolls out of the nest. When this happens, a goose stretches out its neck and hooks the egg back towards the nest with its beak, using a side-to-side movement to keep the egg on course. It keeps doing this until its head is between its legs,

bringing the egg safely back into the nest. Lorenz discovered that if he removed the egg halfway through this procedure, the goose would carry on regardless, as if the egg were still there. The goose could see that the egg was missing, but instinct forced it to finish its stereotyped behaviour, like a computer program that cannot be stopped.

Behavioural routines like this – known as 'fixed action patterns' – are examples of instinct in its purest form. Since Lorenz's research, scientists have discovered that these routines are rare in birds and mammals because these animals learn so much through experience. But the goose's egg retrieval is unlearned and provides a remarkable glimpse of complex behaviour entirely controlled by genes.

BEHAV1OUR THAT
ADDS
UP

Like a real potter, she even tests the quality of the clay, rejecting it if it is too wet, or adding a few drops of moisture from her own saliva if it is too dry.

TAKEN ON THEIR OWN, MANY INSTINCTIVE ROUTINES ARE EXTREMELY SIMPLE. But like separate steps in a computer program, they can add up to make animals behave in amazingly intricate ways. This 'adding up' process explains how beavers build and maintain their dams. It also explains the uncannily complex behaviour of much smaller and simpler creatures, such as water spiders, hermit crabs and female potter wasps.

Potter wasps get their name from their clay nests, which the female builds. Each nest is a masterpiece in miniature – a clay pot, no bigger than a grape, that looks as if it has been thrown on a potter's wheel. To build a pot, the female wasp instinctively heads towards damp, clay-rich soil. She scrapes up mouthfuls of clay in her jaws and ferries them back to the nest site. Here, she adds the clay to the pot and then smoothes it out, continuing until she has created a hollow flask with a narrow neck, topped by a flaring rim. Like a real potter, she even tests the quality of the clay, rejecting it if it is too wet, or adding a few drops of moisture from her own saliva if it is too dry.

Once the pot is complete, a separate set of routines sends the wasp on a very different search. This time, she looks not for clay, but for live caterpillars. She instinctively knows where to look, and what to do when she finds her prey. Grasping a caterpillar with her front legs, she paralyses it with her sting. She then drags it back to the clay nest and, little by little, pushes it in. When the pot is three-quarters full of caterpillars – up to 12 of them – instinct tells her that it is the moment to lay her egg, and her hunting activities come to a stop. Having laid an egg, she seals the nest with an earthen lid. Days or weeks later, the egg hatches into a potter wasp grub and devours the caterpillars.

Underwater architects

Beneath the surface of ponds and ditchwater, the water spider uses the 'adding up' process to create something unique in the animal world. Like all spiders it breathes air, but it feeds on small freshwater animals, including insect grubs, tadpoles and even fish. Some air-breathing animals catch this food by diving, but the water spider lives, hunts and breeds underwater by spinning an air-filled balloon that works like a diving bell.

The water spider's instincts have evolved from those that drive spiders to spin webs on land. The spider chooses a spot in the water among weeds, where it spins a blanket of silk strands into a dome, shaped like a contact lens. When the dome is complete, the spider swims to the surface and uses its hind legs to trap a bubble of air. Paddling hard to overcome the bubble's buoyancy, it dives down and releases the bubble underneath the silk dome. It repeats the process many times as the silk slowly inflates, holding the air in place. When the bell is full, the spider climbs inside and uses it as a lair. If anything edible swims close by, the spider swims out through the bottom of the bell to grasp the victim in its jaws.

The only time water spiders leave the water is when they are very young. At this age, instinct drives them to leave their mother's bell and climb up plant stems into the open air. Here they spin long strands of silk and float away on the breeze – a classic spider technique for spreading far and wide.

Moving home

Hermit crabs live inside discarded shells, so they do not need instincts to tell them how to build a home. But a hermit crab does need to move home as it grows. When this time comes, a complex chain of instincts enables the crab to make the right choice, giving it the best chances of survival.

If empty shells are plentiful, a hermit crab behaves like a human property-buyer, carefully inspecting a dozen shells or more. After finding a likely shell by sight, the crab inspects it with its claws, probing inside to check that the shell is empty. If the shell seems suitable, the crab crawls alongside and rapidly moves out of its existing shell and into the potential replacement. It makes sure that the shell is roomy enough, and that it is the right weight. Heavier shells are stronger, but instinct makes the crab reject those that are too heavy as they require too much energy to carry around. If the new shell fits all the requirements, the temporary move becomes permanent. If not, the crab quickly moves back into its former home and sets off on its search again.

A hermit crab's instincts also tell it how to behave if shells are in short supply. Instead of being choosy, the crab shows a willingness to compromise, accepting shells that it would normally turn down. If many crabs are on the search, suitable shells become highly prized. Driven by their instinct to move

GRUB FOR THE GRUB
After catching a caterpillar, a female potter wasp (above left) carefully pushes it into the pot-shaped clay nest she has built. Here, it will provide food for her grub.

GOOD COMPANIONS This hermit crab is protected by two stinging sea anemones that it has fastened to its shell. It is eating a shrimp – the anemones will share the meal if any small scraps drift their way.

home, hermit crabs often fight over an available shell, and the crab that is strongest gets to move in. Some hermit crabs pick up sea anemones and fasten them to their shells, as the anemones' stings provide the crab with protection from predators. When the crab outgrows its shell and moves into a new one, instinct tells it not to forget its passengers: with some deft movements of its pincers, it moves the anemones, too.

Working together

Instincts that add up can be even more impressive when thousands or millions of animals act together. If a shark threatens a shoal of fish, the shoal suddenly transforms itself into a tunnel so that the shark swims through a fish-free space. When the shark emerges from the tunnel, the shoal instantly regroups and speeds away. Flocks of birds show the same kind of coordination when they are on the move, and so do columns of army ants as they swarm across the forest floor.

From a distance this kind of behaviour gives the impression of real military-style manoeuvres, with a clear chain of command. But in a typical shoal or flock, no single individual is in charge. Instead, each animal reacts in an instinctive way to the behaviour of its nearest neighbours. The outcome is an almost liquid

In a shoal or flock, each animal reacts to the behaviour of its nearest neighbours. The outcome is an almost liquid motion, similar to a football crowd producing a Mexican wave.

motion, similar to a football crowd producing a Mexican wave. The flocking instinct in birds is triggered by vision and hearing. Shoaling instincts in fish are activated by changes in water pressure, which fish sense through organs called lateral lines. These inform a fish how its companions are moving, and instinct tells it which way it should move.

When animals live in large groups, some kinds of behaviour seem to take on a life of their own. For example, a colony of nesting gulls may suddenly be swept by a wave of panic, set off by a single bird sounding the alarm. Each bird is 'infected' by this behaviour, which spreads through the flock like a fire through dry grass. If the alarm turns out to be false, the panic runs out of fuel and the wave of noise gradually fades away.

Another kind of infectious behaviour happens if worker honeybees smell smoke. This triggers them to gorge themselves on honey – the first stage in an instinctive evacuation plan. If the worst comes to the worst and their nest catches fire, this emergency action saves the colony's food. While they are busy feeding, the bees are fully occupied, and their full stomachs makes it hard for them to sting. This is why beekeepers often puff smoke into a hive before they open it up.

INSTINCT IN MOTION A shoal of snappers opens up as a predator heads their way. The fish are all the same size and age, and they instinctively swim a set distance apart.

BEAVER

THE GREATEST BUILDERS IN THE WHOLE
**LIVING WORLD AFTER HUMANS, BEAVERS CONSTRUCT DAMS
THAT DWARF ANYTHING ELSE CREATED BY WILD MAMMALS.**
The largest one on record, straddling the Jefferson River in Montana, USA,
was 700 m long, and strong enough to be used as a bridge by riders on
horseback. This giant dam was exceptional, but even a typical one,
measuring 25 m long, contains the trunks of hundreds of saplings, cut and
trimmed to fit and floated carefully into position.

Beavers build their dams to create a safe habitat for themselves and their young.
Although they spend most of their lives in water, they do not fish – they are vegetarians.
They sometimes eat underwater plants, but most of their food, particularly in winter, consists
of the leaves and bark of waterside trees. Using their powerful incisor teeth, they gnaw through
young trees and drag them into the water. When nearby trees are used up, they dig canals to
reach ones farther away. Not all the wood is used for building dams as some is needed for
building the beavers' quarters – a hollow dome of branches, known as a lodge,
situated in the safety of the lake. The lodge can be over 10 m across and all
its entrances are underwater, beyond the reach of most predators, such as
wolves. Young beavers are born in the lodge, and spend their first two years
with their parents, helping to maintain and extend the lodge and dam.

Beavers are unique among rodents in having a flattened tail, which
works like a combined flipper and rudder. They have webbed hind feet.
When they dive, flaps of skin seal their ears and nostrils. A transparent
inner eyelid, called a nictitating membrane, protects their eyes underwater
and lets them see as they navigate through water, even under ice.

VITAL STATISTICS

CLASS: Mammalia
ORDER: Rodentia
SPECIES: *Castor canadensis*
HABITAT: Rivers and lakes
DISTRIBUTION: North America
KEY FEATURE: Second-largest rodent,
specially adapted for life in water;
builds the largest structures made
by animals, apart from coral reefs

TRIGGERED INTO ACTION

FACE TO FACE Two European robins clash at a well-stocked bird table. The sight of each other's red breasts triggers the robins' aggressive instincts – unless they are a breeding pair.

ACCORDING TO THE PROVERB, IT IS THE EARLY BIRD THAT CATCHES THE WORM. It is also the stealthy bird, because earthworms disappear into the ground within seconds if they are touched. The worm's escape instinct is activated by this special trigger, like a 'go' button telling software to start. To be useful, instinctive behaviour has to happen at the right moment. Earthworms activate their emergency escape when they sense danger, and not at other times. Birds preen their feathers when they are perching, not when they are speeding through the air. The same is true for animals that are newly hatched or newly born: a lion cub starts to suckle the moment it finds its mother's teat, but until that happens its suckling instinct is switched off. The exact trigger varies from one instinct to another, but it ensures that an animal's inbuilt behaviour helps it, instead of wasting energy or – worse still – putting it in harm's way.

Most of the triggers that set off instincts are external changes that an animal can quickly sense. Earthworms cannot see predators approaching because they do not have well-developed eyes. To make up for this, evolution has given them an

In one experiment, tropical motmots raised in captivity were shown models of two different types of snake. They attacked the harmless kind but backed away from the venomous one, although they had never seen a snake before.

escape system that is triggered by their sense of touch. If a worm's tail is touched – even lightly – extra-large nerve fibres flash signals down its body, making its muscles contract. As a result, the worm seems to shrink suddenly, then vanishes underground. Earthworms have another escape instinct, with the reverse effect. If the soil around them vibrates strongly – for example, under the tramp of a gardener's boots – they dig their way up to the surface so that they can escape overground.

ONE FINAL TUG Instincts are not always foolproof. This earthworm started its emergency escape too late, and is likely to end up as the magpie's next meal.

Sight and smell

In many animals, vision plays an important part in triggering instinctive actions. When a resident male European robin spots another male, it attacks the intruder, pecking at it viciously in an attempt to drive it away. Researchers have found that the male's aggressive behaviour is literally an example of 'seeing red', because it is triggered by the sight of the rival's red breast. This trigger works even if the intruder is a painted dummy.

Colours and patterns are common triggers for instinctive behaviour, but instincts can also be triggered by shapes. Young gamebirds instinctively recognise the silhouettes of birds of prey, while many young animals recoil from the sinuous outlines of snakes. Some birds seem to start life knowing which snakes are dangerous and which are not. In one experiment, tropical motmots raised in captivity were shown models of two different types of snake. They attacked the harmless kind but backed away from the venomous one, although they had never seen a snake before.

Birds have a poor sense of smell, but many other animals, particularly insects and mammals, trigger instinctive behaviour among their own kind by releasing special scents. If a honeybee is disturbed or injured, it gives off a substance called isoamyl acetate – the honeybee alarm pheromone. As the scent spreads

through the air, other honeybees speed towards the source, where they surround and sting the attacker. This 'panic alarm' is extremely precise: similar substances with just slightly different chemical structures have no effect on bees at all.

In mammals, scent plays an important part in switching on the instincts involved in breeding. For example, female polar bears rarely encounter males, and if they do they keep their distance because the males are twice their size and highly dangerous. But once every three years a female gives off sex pheromones, showing that she is receptive to males and ready to mate. This airborne trigger is extraordinarily effective in attracting males from miles around.

WHEN INSTINCT BACKFIRES

WHEN ANIMALS' INSTINCTS ARE ACCIDENTALLY SET OFF BY THE WRONG KIND OF TRIGGER, they can behave in strange ways. Whether they are birds pecking at mirrors, or moths flying towards candle flames, they are driven by instincts that they are powerless to resist. In nature, the only place animals see their own reflections is in water that is perfectly flat and calm. But in today's world, urban animals come into contact with reflective surfaces all the time. Birds see themselves in shop windows and the wing-mirrors of cars. Airborne insects see sunshine and moonlight reflected from greenhouses and agricultural plastic as they fly high overhead. These and many other man-made objects can act as accidental triggers for instinctive behaviour.

Animals through the looking glass

Birds are unpredictable when they see themselves face to face. Some species ignore their reflections in mirrors and windows, but others react aggressively, pecking tirelessly at the glass. Male blue tits have been known to die from exhaustion after defending their territory from these 'phantom' intruders that will not go away. This behaviour may seem stupid, but the blue tit is following its internal programme – one that has evolved to run until it is finished, or until the trigger has stopped.

Confronted by a mirror, a kitten will immediately go on the defensive, arching its back and making its fur stand on end. Cats show this behaviour when confronted by any kind of threat, and it has evolved to make them look more dangerous than they really are. But like all carnivorous mammals, kittens learn fast. After passing the mirror a few times, a kitten will look behind it and discover that nothing threatening is lurking there. From this moment on, learned behaviour starts to override instinct. After a few hours, the kitten never makes the same mistake again.

Insects rarely recognise their own reflections, but shiny surfaces confuse them in other ways. Diving beetles often crash into greenhouses on moonlit nights because the glass triggers their instinct to head towards rivers and ponds. Farmers sometimes exploit these instincts to protect their crops: strips of plastic can stop aphids landing because these tiny sap-suckers instinctively keep clear of anything that looks like water.

Danger in the dark

Because they travel at speed, cars pose a danger to many animals. And for some creatures, such as hedgehogs, instinct makes matters worse. Instead of running when confronted by danger, a hedgehog's first instinct is to stop dead in its tracks. If its enemy closes in, the hedgehog raises its spines and rolls up into a ball. These instincts often save a hedgehog's

MISTAKEN IDENTITY Perched on a car's wing mirror, an Australian grey-crowned babbler furiously pecks at its own reflection. The babbler's territorial instincts are triggered by its 'rival' – particularly as it seems to peck back.

life when it is faced by its natural enemies, such as badgers and foxes, but have fatal results when it is faced with an oncoming car.

Instinct and traffic also make a dangerous mix for the barn owl. Found throughout the world, this graceful night-time hunter searches for small mammals using its amazingly keen hearing, which can pick up the faintest sounds. To hunt effectively, the owl flies just a few metres above the ground. Unfortunately, instinct keeps it at this height even if it is in the path of an oncoming vehicle.

Fatal flames

After dark many insects fly towards light, but this instinct can backfire lethally when moths flutter towards flames. Lured by a candle, a moth will spiral around it in ever-decreasing circles until it scorches its wings and drops to the ground. If the light is

behind a glass, the moth will flutter helplessly, as if held there by a spell. Why do moths behave in this bizarre and suicidal way? The answer – most experts believe – is due to the way that moths navigate.

Before humans discovered fire, moths lived in a world where the Moon was the only bright light source at night. Over millions of years, moths evolved a form of navigation that uses the Moon as a reference point. According to this theory, a flying moth instinctively keeps the Moon in the same part of its field of view. Because the Moon is so far away, this makes the moth fly roughly in a straight line. But if the moth does the same thing with a nearby light – such as a candle – the light moves as the moth flies past, and the moth flies in a curve as it tries to keep the light at a steady angle to its eyes. Instead of guiding it on its way, the light lures it closer and closer, until the moth spirals into the flame.

LETHAL DEFENCE Faced by oncoming headlights, a hedgehog stops dead. This 'inappropriate instinct' is responsible for half of all hedgehog deaths in northern Europe, excluding those that occur during hibernation.

THE LURE OF LIGHT Light has a magnetic effect on moths, and scientists use it to capture specimens for study. In tropical forests, over 100 kinds of moth may come fluttering into a brightly lit moth trap during the course of a single night.

1 LAYING THE FOUNDATIONS
A male masked weaver starts its
nest by knotting strips of grass
around a slender branch.

2 COMPLETING THE RING The bird
extends the foundations to form a
ring. It instinctively knows what the
diameter of the ring should be.

3 CONSTRUCTING THE SHELL Working
out from the ring, the bird weaves the
nest wall. It inserts each strip of grass
individually and checks that it is secured.

INSTINCTS AND

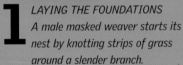

Male weaverbirds know
which building materials
to choose, and when to
stop building because
the job is done. But
instinct does not tell
them where the best
place is to collect
materials, or which is
the quickest route back
to the nest. Those skills
have to be learned.

FOR MALE WEAVERBIRDS, BUILDING A NEST IS A
CRUCIAL PART OF ADULT LIFE BECAUSE FEMALES PICK
THEIR MATES ON THE BASIS OF THE NESTS THEY BUILD.
Instinct tells the males how to weave a nest, but learning
turns them into true masters of their trade. In the animal kingdom,
few creatures – except the very simplest – survive by instinct alone. Instead, most are
like weaverbirds: they learn through experience, adapting to the demands of daily life
and becoming better at what they do.

Basic learning allows animals to ignore things that are alarming but harmless.
Called habituation, it is often described as 'learning what not to do'. For example, the
sound of rustling leaves will make a deer run for cover because it may signal something
dangerous. But if the rustling continues and nothing threatening appears, the deer will
eventually ignore the sound. Birds that attack crops, such as crows and pigeons, are
frightened off when they first see a scarecrow, but after several hours they behave as if it
is not there. Lions and cheetahs behave in a similar way in busy parts of Africa's national
parks. To them, cars are part of the scenery, even though they move. Habituation saves
animals enormous amounts of time and energy by allowing them to ignore false alarms.
Their escape instincts are still intact and are back in charge if a threat turns out to be real.

From novice to expert
For nest-building weaverbirds, the balance between instinct and learning works in a
subtle way. Most weaverbirds are polygamous, with males making several nests for
several partners during the course of the breeding season. Females play no part in

4 *EXTENDING THE ENTRANCE The shell is complete, and the bird starts on the downward-pointing entrance, which consists of a short tube.*

LEARNING

nest-building – instead they make the choice, and they look for nests that are well woven and recently built. Such nests hold together during the rainy season, until the female's brood has hatched and her young are ready to fly.

When male weavers make a nest, they instinctively know how to build the foundations by weaving grass into a ring. Instinct also tells them how to build the spherical shell and the tubular entrance that helps to prevent predators getting in. They know which building materials to choose, and when to stop building because the job is done. But instinct does not tell them where the best place is to collect materials, or which is the quickest route back to the nest. Those skills have to be learned.

A well-crafted nest made of fresh grass lures females, like a brand-new show-home. A badly woven nest made of old grass attracts far less attention; and as time goes by it becomes increasingly unkempt until instinct tells its builder to start again.

Heading south

While instinct plays a large part in the behaviour of simple animals, complex instincts can have far-reaching effects in animals with well-developed brains. One remarkable example is the European cuckoo, which lays its eggs in other birds' nests. When a young cuckoo hatches, instinct drives it to push against the other eggs with the small of its back until they have all tumbled out of the nest. It then receives all the food collected by its unwitting foster parents. Instinct is even more impressive when the cuckoo is ready to fly. By this time, its real parents have already departed for their winter home in southern Africa. Driven by instinct, the young cuckoo follows the same course, travelling thousands of miles on its own to a place it has never seen before.

HOMES ON DISPLAY The male hangs beneath the nest and flutters his wings to invite females to inspect it. Above the nest is another one, also waiting for a female to move in.

CULTURE CLUB

One female – called Imo – washed her food first in a stream. Within weeks, other monkeys were copying her example, and within ten years, almost all of the monkeys apart from the very young and the very old washed their food.

UNLIKE INSTINCT, LEARNED BEHAVIOUR IS NOT INHERITED WHEN LIVING THINGS BREED, but it can be passed on as animals copy their own kind. This way of acquiring skills – supremely important in the human world – is also used by some animals in the wild. When a fox cub follows its mother and watches her while she hunts, it learns how to put its own hunting instincts to work. The same is true when a chick follows a hen and pecks at the same things as its mother. But some animals – particularly primates – can pass on completely new skills in this way. With this kind of learning, it is not simply who you are that counts, and whose genes you inherit. Behaviour can jump generations and across families.

TABLE MANNERS In the animal world, like the human one, good ideas sometimes catch on. This Japanese macaque has learned to rinse its food before eating it by watching other macaques do the same thing. Primates are very good at copying each other, and this helps them to pass on new skills.

INSTINCT AND EXPERIENCE
This gecko has discovered a
perfect place to hunt for
insects – near an outside light.
Instinct drives the gecko to find
food, but does not tell it exactly
where to look – the gecko
learns this by experience.

In one famous incident in 1953, scientists were present at the very moment when an example of skill-sharing began. It happened on Koshima Island, Japan, where researchers were studying the behaviour of Japanese macaques. To lure the monkeys out of the forest, the research team scattered pieces of sweet potato on the beach. Most of the monkeys picked up the food and ate it, even though it was covered with sand. However, one female – called Imo – washed her food in a stream before eating it. Within weeks, other monkeys were copying her example, and within ten years, almost all of the monkeys apart from the very young and the very old washed their food.

Imo's discovery probably came about by chance, and scientists now doubt that she was the only macaque ever to have made this breakthrough. But on Koshima, the spread of food-washing among the macaques showed very graphically how a useful discovery can catch on.

Following the tradition

In Europe, researchers have found an intriguing example of copycat behaviour in birds. European oystercatchers eat a wide range of food, but those that tackle mussels get at their food in one of two ways. Some birds, nicknamed 'stabbers', use their beaks to pry open mussel shells and cut the tough ligaments that join the two halves. Others, known as 'hammerers', take a more direct approach, using their beaks to smash their way in. Adult birds can be either a stabber or a hammerer, but never both. As they age, each kind develops a slightly different beak because they have different patterns of wear.

Young oystercatchers do not instinctively know how to open mussels; they have to learn. They can become either a stabber or a hammerer – their basic pecking instinct gives them the potential for both. But while they are fledglings, the adult

birds around them set the example and they nearly always follow suit, adopting their local 'tradition' and becoming part of the same cultural club. The proof that this is not inherited comes if chicks from hammering parents and stabbing parents are swapped. If a chick from stabbing parents is brought up by a pair of hammerers, it adopts their habits and becomes a hammerer itself.

Learning and luck

In nature, animals learn new behaviour in different ways. Trial-and-error learning happens in all animals, whereas learning by imitation happens only in those that live in groups. But imitation is a difficult thing to prove and scientists are always cautious when talking about animals copying each other. This is because copying can sometimes be trial-and-error in disguise.

A nocturnal lizard called the house gecko shows how blurred the boundaries are. The house gecko's natural habitat is forest, but many are found living in buildings, where they run up walls and even across ceilings thanks to their sticky toes. House geckos are often found close to lights, where they prey on moths and other insects attracted there after dark. In the wild, geckos never see bright lights, so how do they learn that brightly lit walls are good places to hunt?

One explanation is that they learn by example. Compared to most lizards, geckos are sociable animals with a noisy repertoire of croaks and squeaks. If one gecko sees another hunting near a light, it may move in as well. But instinct makes geckos naturally inquisitive animals, always on the lookout for good places to hunt. If they do not find out about lights from other geckos, it is quite likely that they will make the lucky discovery for themselves. For them, as for most animals, instinct and learning form a complex package – one that can be very difficult to tease apart.

RHYTHMS OF LIFE

2

AS EVENING FALLS, A STREAM OF BATS – MORE THAN A MILLION OF THEM – COMES POURING OUT OF THE CARLSBAD CAVERNS in New Mexico to feed on flying insects high in the sky. The bats roost in total darkness, but each instinctively knows when the day outside has come to an end. Within as little as 30 minutes of nightfall, the adult bats leave their young and flock out of the caves to feed, creating a giant swarm that spirals upwards on fast-beating, leathery wings. Freetail bats are not alone in being able to sense the passage of time. Throughout the living world all kinds of animals, from songbirds to salmon, keep in step with nature's rhythms thanks to their inbuilt biological clocks. The secrets of this timekeeping ability are still not fully understood, but what is known can throw a revealing light on the way we behave as well.

KEEPING IN STEP

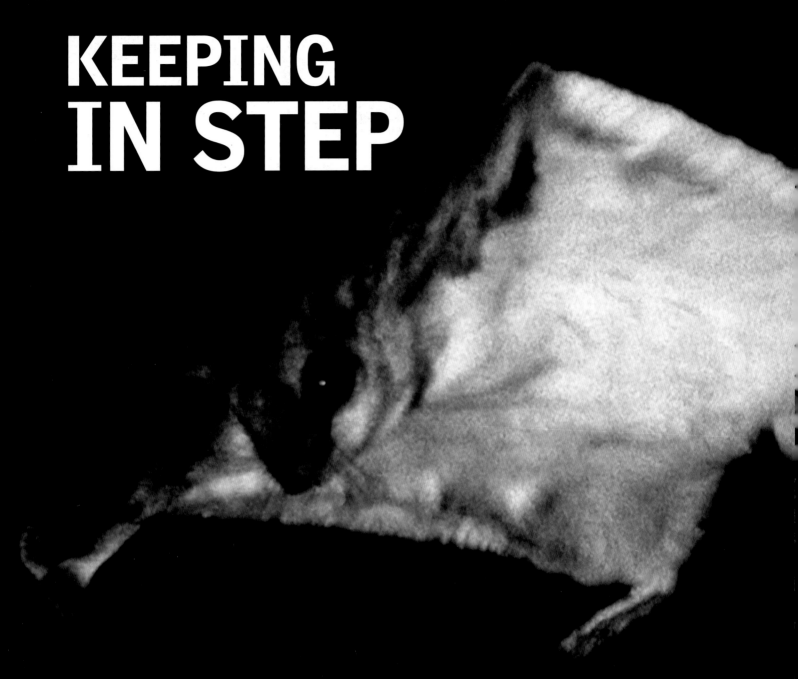

LEAP INTO THE DARK For flying squirrels, darkness is an ally because there are fewer flying predators on the move. These large-eyed rodents come to life at dusk, woken by an internal 'alarm clock' that keeps them in step with the cycle of day and night. Non-flying squirrels are exactly the opposite: night is their time to sleep.

ANIMALS DO NOT HAVE CALENDARS, DIARIES OR WATCHES, but they can be uncannily good at keeping in step with the passing of time in the world around them. Many creatures follow the rhythms of day and night or the changing seasons, and a few show an amazing ability to 'count' much longer periods – up to a decade or more. For most animals – even the very simplest – the ability to keep in step with nature's rhythms is a vital part of survival. It ensures that they find the most food, breed at the best time and, as far as possible, avoid hazards such as summer drought or winter cold. This natural time-keeping confers such a huge advantage that it has evolved in countless different animals and in many different forms.

Hidden triggers

Humans are diurnal, waking when it is light and sleeping when it is dark. Many animals are the opposite, being at their most active after dark. These nocturnal animals include the majority of the world's mammals, some birds, many insects and the vast and varied collection of drifting creatures that make up animal plankton in the seas. At night, planktonic animals feed close to the water's surface, but as dawn breaks they instinctively migrate downwards. This daily migration helps them to avoid plankton-eating fish, which hunt near the surface during daylight hours.

At first it would seem obvious that the changeovers between the day and night shifts are controlled entirely by the Sun. But it is more complicated than this. The behaviour of many animals follows a diurnal or nocturnal pattern even if they are kept in constant daylight or constant darkness. A similar response is seen in many animals that usually follow other

external rhythms, such as the seasons or the tides. The explanation for this is a surprising one: instead of responding directly to nature's rhythms, many animals respond to an internal rhythm, or 'biological clock'.

Keeping track

On the windswept islands of the Southern Ocean, the king penguin shows how instinctive rhythms sometimes override those set by nature. This impressive bird – second only to the emperor penguin in size – follows a unique breeding timetable, raising a chick about once every 18 months. The cycle starts during the subantarctic spring, typically in November, when a nesting pair lays a single egg. The chick takes over a year to become independent, and the parents do not lay their next egg until nearly a year and a half after the previous one, typically in February during the rapidly shortening days of late summer. Although winter is just around the corner, their biological clock triggers off their breeding behaviour so that the next egg can be laid. When that chick has been raised, the rhythm has turned full circle and the parents can once again breed in spring.

Penguins are long-lived birds, so they can breed many times. In the insect world life is very different. Many insects spend most of their lives as larvae or grubs, and breed just once

when adult. For these animals, growing up follows strict timetables set by biological clocks. For example, in most mayfly species 'childhood' lasts a year. Then the young mayfly crawls out of its watery home in a river or lake and takes to the air for an adult life that lasts less than one day.

Many insects have yearly life cycles, although few are as lopsided as the mayfly's. For many larger insects, such as stag beetles, the clock ticks more slowly, and life can last for more than five years. For the periodical cicadas of the eastern USA, it lasts even longer. These plump, bug-eyed insects hold the record for the longest synchronised life cycle anywhere in the animal world, including a childhood phase of 13-17 years, which they spend underground feeding on tree roots (see pages 38 and 39).

PASSAGE TO ADULTHOOD After a childhood spent underground, a periodical cicada sheds its skin for a final time, to take up life as an adult.

BIOLOGICAL CLOCKS

FOUR WEEKS AFTER HATCHING FROM ITS EGG, A MONARCH CATERPILLAR COMPLETES A BREATHTAKING TRANSFORMATION INTO A BRILLIANTLY COLOURED ADULT BUTTERFLY. Like the rest of the monarch's development, an on-board biological clock triggers this change. Animals have several of these inbuilt clocks, each controlling different aspects of behaviour and development. Chemical reactions triggered by the release of hormones from the brain control the different behaviours, but the exact details of how this works are still far from clear.

Hormones play a key part in the monarch butterfly's development. After the caterpillar hatches, it grows rapidly as it feeds. Every few days it sheds its skin, or moults, and grows another one. Each time this happens the caterpillar increases in size, but its overall shape stays the same. After the fifth moult, something remarkable happens. The caterpillar loses its appetite, stops feeding and turns into a chrysalis. About seven days later, the chrysalis splits open to reveal an adult butterfly. Once its wings have dried, it flies away.

A substance called juvenile hormone literally keeps a caterpillar young. As long as enough juvenile hormone is produced, the caterpillar remains a caterpillar every time it sheds its skin. Only after the fifth moult does it turn first into a chrysalis, then into an adult butterfly.

Childhood's end

For centuries, naturalists have been fascinated by the way a caterpillar's body is broken down and then rebuilt. But it took a 20th-century discovery to explain how the change is brought about. In the 1940s, scientists discovered that a caterpillar's brain produces a hormone called ecdysone, which triggers its body to moult. At the same time, it releases a substance called juvenile hormone, which literally keeps it young. As long as enough juvenile hormone is produced, the caterpillar remains a caterpillar every time it sheds its skin. However, the supply of juvenile hormone gradually wanes and after the fifth moult there is no longer enough to prevent metamorphosis. The caterpillar first turns into a chrysalis, and then into an adult butterfly.

Juvenile hormone is found in all insects. At the beginning of the life cycle it is present in high levels; it then drops to the point at which the larva pupates and becomes an adult. In monarch butterflies, this process takes about four weeks – the time needed for the caterpillar to eat enough food to build an adult butterfly. But in periodical cicadas (see page 37), the process takes an incredible 13 or 17 years, depending on the species. At the end of this time, all the cicadas in the same region become adults simultaneously. They climb up trees and

screech loudly to attract a mate, creating a deafening barrage of sound. In the long gaps between, there is silence, because there are no adult cicadas and all the young ones are underground.

No one really knows why periodical cicadas have evolved such a strange and precise natural rhythm. The most likely explanation is that it is a way of dealing with predators. By emerging in such huge numbers, they swamp their enemies. Many are eaten, but the huge majority mate successfully and lay their eggs. Once that task is over, their job is complete and they die.

Clocks that drift

The periodical cicada's clock is doubly remarkable because it hardly ever drifts out of time. Most other biological clocks can be affected by outside factors, such as temperature. The warmer the temperature, the faster the insect grows up. The difference can be remarkable: when the temperature is 15°C, fruit flies take about 30 days to complete their life cycle. When it is 30°C, their clock speed is around four times faster.

Biological clocks also need occasional resetting. This process is called entrainment, and it uses external cues to keep the clock on time. For nocturnal animals, such as flying squirrels, the cue is dawn and dusk. If a flying squirrel is kept in constant darkness, it still splits its time into 'day' and 'night', but its clock runs slightly fast, turning full circle every 23 hours. Humans are the opposite – if people are kept in constant light, their cycle of waking and sleeping is 25 hours long.

BIRTH OF A BUTTERFLY A monarch butterfly emerges from its chrysalis, completing a process that is timed and triggered by a biological clock.

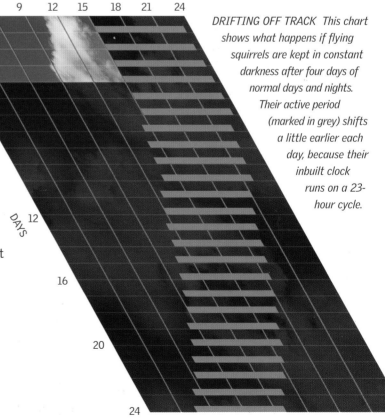

DRIFTING OFF TRACK This chart shows what happens if flying squirrels are kept in constant darkness after four days of normal days and nights. Their active period (marked in grey) shifts a little earlier each day, because their inbuilt clock runs on a 23-hour cycle.

HOURS

3   6   9   12   15   18   21   24

DAYS

1

4

8

12

16

20

24

INBUILT RHYTHMS

WHEN THE SUN RISES ON A SUMMER'S DAY, A DRAGONFLY PREPARES FOR THE HUNT. Once it is airborne, it uses its outsized eyes to spot other flying insects, and instinct helps it to outmanoeuvre its victims as it closes in for the kill. This kind of coordination is possible only because its body is controlled by fast-moving electrical signals flashing along nerves to and from its brain. Thanks to this natural wiring, the dragonfly can dart forwards with pinpoint precision, dive backwards or even hover in midair.

But in an animal's body, not everything is under this kind of direct control. There are some rhythmic activities that work semiautomatically, and others that are endogenous, meaning that they are inbuilt features of living cells, which need no external supervision at all. Endogenous rhythmic activities include breathing, heartbeat and a special kind of insect flight.

AERIAL ASSAULT Dragonflies are exceptionally agile on the wing – a skill that they use to snatch other insects in midair. Their wing muscles are housed in an extra-large thorax, which bulges behind a dragonfly's head.

A breath of air

Breathing is something that we do all the time, without having to think when to do it. Other animals with lungs work in the same way, and the smaller they are, the faster they breathe in and out. An elephant's cavernous lungs fill up about four times a minute, but a hummingbird's have to work much faster. Even at rest, a hummingbird takes about 250 breaths a minute, and when it hovers, the rate can reach 500 breaths or more. Hummingbirds have to breathe this rapidly because they need lots of oxygen to hover, but they have tiny lungs that hold only a minute amount of air. We humans can choose to breathe quickly or slowly – the average rate when we are at rest is about 15 breaths per minute – but with animals this vital rhythm works without any conscious control.

Diving animals – such as gannets and other seabirds – instinctively shut off their breathing before they plunge beneath the water's surface. A young gannet does not have to learn to do this. Instead, instinct takes control, allowing the bird to plunge from dizzying heights without the risk of getting water in its lungs. Although humans are land animals, we have similar reflexes: at moments of potential danger, a particularly powerful reflex makes us hold our breath.

Insects on autopilot

Dragonflies beat their wings up to 25 times a second, and they can fine-tune the rate to alter their speed. But in many smaller insects, such as mosquitoes and midges, flapping wings have a built-in rhythm of their own. Once they start up, a mosquito's wings beat nearly 1000 times every second and, unlike a dragonfly's, they run on autopilot, without any direct control from the insect's brain.

Instead of being connected to flight muscles, wings like these are connected directly to the middle section of an insect's body case, or thorax. One set of muscles pulls in the sides of the thorax, making them click in and out like the lid of a can. Another side pulls in the top and bottom, making them click up and down. When one set pulls, the other set is stretched, triggering it to pull in turn. The result is a self-perpetuating, ultrafast movement – one that makes a mosquito's wings beat with their characteristic high-pitched whine.

When a mosquito touches down, its wings automatically shut down so that it can start to feed. If it loses contact with its victim, even for a split second, it instinctively starts to fly again. Its legs work like a switch mechanism, making sure that its wings keep working as long as it is in the air.

Some of the deepest divers, such as seals and whales, do exactly the opposite. They take several deep breaths, loading their bodies with oxygen, but then breathe out before disappearing beneath the waves. This instinct prevents the air being squeezed by the tremendous pressure of deep water – something that could make their lungs burst.

Beating hearts

In the animal kingdom, rhythms work on every imaginable scale, from the level of the shoal or herd right down to individual cells. Many animal cells have their own rhythms, but none is more vital than the steady beat of muscle cells in the heart. These cells contract according to their own built-in rhythm, almost as if they had nervous systems of their own. They keep doing this, even if they are isolated and kept alive in a laboratory dish.

Like breathing, heart rate is directly linked to an animal's size. The rate speeds up when the animal is active, but it always drops back again when the animal is at rest. An elephant's heart rate is about 25 beats a minute, about a third of the rate of an adult human's. The blue whale holds the record for the slowest rate: about eight beats a minute, or one every seven seconds. Its heart is the largest in the animal world, weighing over half a tonne. It pumps more than 10 000 litres of blood around the whale's body – about 2000 times more than the volume pumped by a human heart, and nearly a million times more than a shrew's.

An elephant's heart rate is about 25 beats a minute, about a third of the rate of an adult human's. The blue whale holds the record for the slowest rate: about eight beats a minute, or one every seven seconds.

Shutting down for winter

The heart's built-in rhythm is the ultimate fail-safe system, ensuring that nothing impedes its work. But in some animals the heart switches to a special 'low gear' when the time comes to hibernate. Instinct triggers hibernation, and when it starts, the animal's body temperature and heart rate both tumble. A hibernating bat's heart rate can be as slow as five beats a minute – just enough to keep its chilled body alive. When spring arrives and the bat wakes, the heart is one of the first organs to warm up. As the heart picks up speed, it pumps more oxygen around the bat's body and, little by little, the bat begins to stir and comes back to life.

BODY MASS AND HEART RATE

Small mammals, such as shrews, have tiny hearts that beat hundreds of times a minute. An elephant's heart beats much more slowly, but with an enormous force.

ANIMAL	BODY MASS (grams)	HEART RATE (beats per minute)
Shrew	3	600
Rat	200	420
Guinea pig	300	300
Rabbit	2000	200
Dog (large)	30 000	85
Human	70 000	72
Horse	450 000	38
Elephant	3 000 000	25

TIMETABLES OF LIFE

NATURAL RHYTHMS AFFECT LIFE IN ALMOST ALL HABITATS, INCLUDING THE DEEPEST, DARKEST CAVES. In order to make the most of their surroundings, and keep in touch with their own kind, animals have instinctive timetables that help them to fit in with these rhythms.

Dawn is not good for finding food because the light is faint, but it is a good time for attracting attention because the air is often still. To human ears, the dawn chorus is tuneful and relaxing, but for birds it contains urgent messages, best broadcast at the start of the day.

GREETING THE DAWN Perched on a fencepost, a North American dickcissel broadcasts its morning call. Male dickcissels often sing right through the winter.

DAILY RHYTHMS

FOR MANY CREATURES, DAILY RHYTHMS ARE THE MOST IMPORTANT, ALTHOUGH INBUILT TIMETABLES ALSO TAKE ACCOUNT OF LUNAR RHYTHMS AND SEASONAL CHANGE. The only exception is in the oceans' greatest depths, where there are no days and nights, no seasons and few changes of any kind – here and here alone, time seems to stand still. Elsewhere, rhythms rule. From tropical rain forests to temperate woodlands, the sounds of diurnal animals starting a new day greet the dawn. In the forests of South-east Asia, the haunting calls of gibbons ring out over the treetops, while in temperate woodlands, songbirds produce a chorus of sound. For both gibbons and birds, these calls serve the same purpose: they announce who is where.

The dawn chorus of songbirds starts as soon as the eastern sky begins to show the first faint hint of light. Different birds start up at different times: in northern Europe, the first to sing are often robins and blackbirds, followed by tits and finches. Once the day has fully broken the chorus subsides, but it is often followed by a second, more muted chorus as the day ends and birds prepare to roost. The dawn chorus is much louder in spring than at other times of year, because male birds use song to attract females and keep rivals away.

But why do birds instinctively sing so loudly at dawn, instead of later in the day? The most likely explanation – according to most ornithologists – is that it makes best use of their time. Dawn is not good for finding food because the light is faint, but it is a good time for attracting attention because the air is often still. To human ears, the chorus is tuneful and relaxing, but for birds it contains urgent messages – ones that are best broadcast at the start of the day.

NO TIME TO LOSE A pygmy shrew is dwarfed by its earthworm prey. Tiny but ferocious, shrews have to hunt day and night to fuel their high-energy lifestyle. Scaled up to human size, the smallest kinds would eat up to a quarter of a tonne of food every 24 hours.

The daily round

Many animals instinctively follow the same daily routine. For meerkats in the desert scrub of southern Africa, the day starts about an hour after the Sun has risen. One at a time, the meerkats emerge from their communal burrow and devote the next hour or more to sunbathing, grooming and keeping a watchful eye on their surroundings. Finally, one of the group heads off, and the rest follow to begin the day's hunt. They take a different route each day and rest in the heat of the early afternoon. Eventually, they turn back again, reaching their burrow before sunset. After resting in the waning light, they disappear underground for the night.

A meerkat can sleep through the night because it has enough food stored in its body to keep it going. But for pygmy shrews – among the world's smallest mammals – a good night's sleep is not an option. Weighing as little as 3 g, pygmy shrews are entirely carnivorous, and their bodies are like tiny furnaces that need a constant supply of fuel. If a pygmy shrew goes for more than four hours without a meal, it runs out of fuel and dies. This precarious balancing act explains why shrews are active around the clock. It is not daylight and darkness that controls their lives, but hunger – an instinct they cannot afford to ignore.

For cold-blooded animals, such as reptiles and insects, daily life is much more dependent on climatic conditions. The savanna monitor – a 1 m long lizard from Africa's grasslands – needs warmth to become active, so its spends the early hours of the day basking in the Sun. By mid-morning its body warms up and it sets off to hunt. By early afternoon, however, overheating can become a problem, and if this happens the monitor instinctively heads for the shade. It hunts again in the late afternoon, and then, as the air starts to cool, it returns to its lair for the night.

Butterflies behave in a similar way, spreading their wings as the Sun rises to catch the maximum amount of warmth. They cannot take off until they have soaked up enough heat, and they stay grounded if the weather turns unusually cold. Bumblebees, by contrast, can warm themselves. Using their wing muscles, they shiver for several minutes before takeoff, raising their temperature until it is up to 15°C higher than the chilly morning air. Using this system, bumblebees in the Arctic can start flying as early as 3 am – the earliest start for a bee anywhere in the world.

COLLECTING DEW After a night spent on a coastal sand dune, a Namib darkling beetle is decked with droplets of dew. It drinks the droplets by tilting its body, so that they roll towards its mouth.

One insect, the Namib darkling beetle, depends on cool damp conditions to survive. It lives in the Namib coastal desert, where the only reliable moisture is the thick sea fog that rolls inland every night. As darkness falls, the beetle makes its way to the top of a dune, where it collects droplets of water that condense on its body. As dawn breaks, and the fog begins to clear, it finishes the last remaining droplets and then quickly scuttles away.

Night rhythms

For nocturnal animals, dusk marks the start of another day. Their biological clocks wake them as the Sun sets, or earlier in places where summer nights are short. Fewer animals are active by night than by day, but even so, the natural world is full of activity after dark. Owls and nightjars come out to feed, and much more importantly, so do the majority of the world's mammal species. Out of a total of some 4500 mammal species, well over half are nocturnal, including small primates such as the tarsier, a bewildering assortment of rodents, the majority of carnivores and every single one of the world's 977 types of bat.

Well over half of mammal species are nocturnal, including small primates such as the tarsier, many rodents, most carnivores and every single one of the world's 977 types of bat.

Instinct organises animals' nightly timetables in different ways. Once a barn owl has woken up, it will often spend the whole night hunting, retuning to its roost in the pale light of dawn. Bats are much more varied. Some kinds leave their roost promptly at dusk, while others wait until the night is well under way. Fruit-eating species often stay out until sunrise, while some insect-eaters can be back at their roost by midnight and will stay there until making a final flight just before dawn. Their nocturnal 'siesta' at the dead of night helps them to digest their initial catch before setting off for more.

Night visitors

During the breeding season, some animals – particularly seabirds – use the cover of darkness to return to their nests. Shearwaters breed on remote cliff-tops, where they land clumsily on the turf, while tiny storm petrels, which are not much bigger than sparrows, flutter ashore on remote islands and rocky coasts.

All these birds have weak feet and shuffle rather than walk. This makes them very vulnerable to predators, and instinct keeps them at sea during daylight hours so they avoid the gulls and skuas that lurk on land. Even moonlit nights can be dangerous: if the Moon is very bright, they stay out at sea, waiting until the following night before trying their luck again.

The sleepers

Meanwhile, as nature's night shift continues, diurnal animals are asleep. Sleep has its own rhythms – ones that vary enormously from one animal to another. Seals sleeping on pack ice in the Arctic often doze in quick snatches of no more than a few minutes each, because they are instinctively aware of the danger posed by polar bears. Antelope seldom

*BIG EYES In the forests of
Indonesia, the tarsier uses its
enormous eyes to pinpoint insects
in bushes and trees.*

*HEADING HOME A barn owl returns to its
nest with a vole in its beak. Barn owls do not
need light to hunt – they can find their prey
entirely by sound.*

*FAMILY OUTING European badgers usually
wait until dusk before coming out of their
burrows. If they are on the move in daylight
it is usually a sign that food is short.*

risk more than a few minutes with their eyes closed. But
roosting songbirds can sleep for several hours at a time.
A special mechanism stops them falling off their perches:
when they settle, their weight makes their toes lock into
position and the toes stay like this until they wake up.

The most extraordinary sleepers spend the whole
night on the wing. As dusk falls, flocks of common swifts
fly upwards and eventually disappear from sight. At one
time, ornithologists assumed that they landed after dark,
but radar tracking shows that they stay aloft, at heights
of up to 2000 m. They presumably spend some of their
time asleep, but researchers do not know exactly how
they stay airborne as they doze.

LUNAR RHYTHMS

ON COASTS AND ESTUARIES, TIDES DOMINATE LIFE. Like day and night, the tides run to a precise timetable – one set by the position of the Moon and Sun. Every 12 hours, the tide rises, falls, then rises again as the Earth rotates and the Moon moves across the sky. In addition, the tide's total sweep changes over a 29-day period, as Moon and Sun line up on opposite sides of the Earth, then move apart. This produces a double set of rhythms, which sometimes reinforce each other, sometimes cancel each other out. Modern computers can predict tides almost anywhere on Earth. But thanks to their inherited instincts, animals have been keeping in step with these tidal rhythms for millions of years.

Feeding with the tide

Every time the tide rises, it brings food to animals fastened to the shore. Barnacles open their shells as soon as they are submerged, but most seashore molluscs – such as mussels and oysters – do

APPOINTMENT WITH THE TIDE On North America's east coast, primeval-looking horseshoe crabs scuttle ashore on a high spring tide to mate.

not respond to the water itself. They open their shells, but time their opening hours according to an inbuilt 'tidal clock', and they stick doggedly to this rhythm. Although their clock drifts, they will keep opening and closing for several days, even if they are kept in a tideless tank and moved far inland.

When the tide falls, mussels and oysters close up their shells, and a different set of creatures comes out to feed. Wading birds probe the mud with their sensitive beaks, and crabs emerge from their burrows. In tropical mangrove swamps, fiddler crabs sidle along the banks of muddy creeks, picking up tiny particles of food with their claws. Their tidal clock runs about six hours behind an oyster's, so instinct ushers them back to their burrows before the tide returns.

Journey ashore

Nature's clock also keeps seashore animals in step with the 29-day rhythm of the lunar month. Twice every 29 days, when the Moon and Sun are aligned, extra-large 'spring' tides reach unusually far up the shore. For many animals – from corals to horseshoe crabs – this is the perfect moment to spawn.

Following the call of instinct, horseshoe crabs gather in the shallows, where they can follow the water as it rises up the beach. When the tide reaches it height, millions emerge from the sea to mate and lay their eggs just beyond the reach of the waves. Their eggs hatch in time to catch another extra-high tide, which sweeps the tiny crab larvae out into the vastness of the sea.

MARMOT

MARMOTS ARE CHAMPION HIBERNATORS.

IN PLACES WITH MILD CLIMATES, THEY HIBERNATE FOR AS LITTLE AS EIGHT WEEKS, BUT THEY SPEND UP TO NINE MONTHS tucked up underground in colder regions, such as central Asia and Siberia, leaving themselves just three months in which to find a whole year's supply of food.

Marmots live both in high mountains and on open grassland, feeding on a diet of grasses and other plants. They carry grass underground to line their nests, but unlike many rodents they do not store food. Instead, they feed around the clock in late spring and early summer and build up a large amount of body fat. This fat accounts for up to half their weight by summer, and they use it as fuel during the long sleep. Even so, hibernation is a dangerous time, especially for the young. If a marmot does not build up enough fat, it risks starving to death before it has a chance to start feeding again in spring.

Altogether, there are 14 species of these appealing rodents, which are closely related to prairie dogs. Four kinds live in North America; the rest are found in Europe and northern Asia.

VITAL STATISTICS

CLASS: Mammalia
ORDER: Rodentia
SPECIES: *Marmota* species
DISTRIBUTION: Temperate regions of the Northern Hemisphere
HABITAT: Mountain pastures or windswept steppes
KEY FEATURES: Burrowing herbivorous rodent with sharp, gnawing teeth; in cold regions has the longest hibernation time of any mammal.

YEARLY RHYTHMS

AT THE EQUATOR, EVERY DAY IS ALMOST EXACTLY 12 HOURS LONG. But farther north and south, day length changes as one season follows another. At a latitude of 40° – level with New York in the Northern Hemisphere – the days are nine hours long in midwinter and 15 hours long in midsummer. Farther north still, beyond the Arctic Circle, the difference is even greater. The Sun never rises in December, and in June it never sets. Unlike changes in the weather, these changes in day length are completely dependable because they follow exactly the same pattern year after year. This explains why changes in day length trigger instinctive behaviour in a lot of animals. And for many of them, the most important periods in the calendar are early autumn and early spring.

Advance preparations

In early autumn, as the days start to shorten, sockeye salmon migrate up the rivers of Alaska, Canada and the western USA, heading towards the very same lakes where they hatched out

AUTUMN JOURNEY In a Canadian river, brightly coloured sockeye salmon near the end of their journey to their spawning grounds.

from eggs up to seven years earlier. Their navigation is instinctive, and so is their timing, which allows them to spawn in time for their eggs to hatch in spring. In many rivers and streams, this autumn 'run' occurs within the same short period each year, and the water seems to churn and boil as the salmon push onwards against the current, not stopping even to feed.

The shortening days of autumn also trigger hibernation in mammals and restlessness in migratory birds. As the weeks go by, increasing numbers of long-distance travellers reach the point where instinct nudges them to depart. But as with daily rhythms, this annual rhythm is not always triggered by external factors. Many birds have an inbuilt 'annual clock' that keeps them in step with the seasons. Even those that are kept in indoor aviaries get ready for migration right on time.

The baby boom

The coldest weather in winter usually comes well after the shortest day. But whatever the weather, the amount of daylight grows steadily, reaching its fastest increase at the equinox – the official start of spring. In the temperate world, this is when nature really starts to get into gear after its winter calm.

Unlike humans, lots of mammal species are locked into breeding cycles that are centred on spring. Grey wolves, for example, mate in late winter, and their cubs are born about 63 days later, in early spring. After that, no more cubs are born until the following year unless something happens to the male and female pair that lead the pack. Songbirds are even more tied to

the calendar. During autumn and winter their reproductive systems shrink – to save energy and weight. At that time of year they are physically incapable of mating or laying eggs. But as the days lengthen in spring, the process goes into reverse, and the annual round of courtship and breeding begins.

Seizing the opportunity

Not all animals follow the calendar as closely as sockeye salmon or wolves. In places with unpredictable climates, such as deserts, instinct turns animals into opportunists, always ready to take advantage of a favourable turn in the weather.

This is the lifestyle followed by several of Australia's best-known birds, including the black swan and the Australian pelican. These two waterbirds instinctively follow rain, gathering in their hundreds or even thousands in places where sudden storms create temporary lakes. Their breeding behaviour switches on straightaway, allowing them to raise their young before the water dries up and they have to move on.

NUZZLING MOTHER Grey wolf cubs playing with their mother in Montana, USA. They are born at a time of year when food is beginning to be plentiful again.

TAKING ADVANTAGE Australia's black swans breed whenever and wherever they can. Here, large numbers have gathered on the shallow waters of Lake Wollumboola in New South Wales.

THE MA
IMPERA

TING
TIVE
3

A PAIR OF JAPANESE CRANES PERFORM THEIR ELABORATE MATING DANCE ON AN ICE-COVERED LAKE. With wings held half open, they bob their heads and bow down low, then leap high into the air. This exuberant ceremony is carried out by cranes of all ages, but it is particularly important for young adults, which display to each other before they mate. Like all animals, cranes are driven by the instinct to reproduce. This is the most powerful force in the animal world, ensuring that species endure and adapt by passing on their genes. For all but the simplest animals, reproduction depends on finding a mate – a difficult and potentially dangerous mission. Some animals have many partners, but cranes have just one; they are revered in Japan as symbols of fidelity, longevity and happiness. For them, the right choice is vital because the bond lasts for life.

INSTINCT VERSUS INSTINCT

INTENSE MOMENT A male leopard, photographed in South Africa's Mala Mala game reserve, grips his partner by the neck while he mates with her. Leopards mate dozens of times over a period of a few days, and then go separate ways.

REPRODUCTION IS THE MOST IMPORTANT TASK IN ANY ANIMAL'S LIFE. In most species two parents are needed, and both have to behave in exactly the right way if the outcome is to be a success. When a pair of animals get ready to reproduce, two powerful instincts meet in a head-on clash. The first is the instinct to find a partner. The second is the aggressive instinct – the normal response of most animals when a stranger gets too close.

In tigers, leopards and other cats, aggression often seems to get the upper hand. Cat courtship can be a noisy business, and it starts with the female calling loudly – a signal that often attracts several males. If this happens, the rivals fight for the right to mate. Female cats are receptive for only a few days each year, so instinct spurs on the males in their contest to be a successful suitor. Fights are ferocious and injuries can be serious, or even fatal.

When one male has triumphed, he still has the female to contend with. Instead of encouraging him, she is more likely to lash out with her claws, stopping him from getting near. But this apparent hostility is a normal part of cat courtship, and it disappears over the course of several days. Finally, the female accepts the male's advances. She crouches down, stays still and allows him to mate. In many cats, the male bites the female on the scruff of the neck, but instinct stops him causing her serious harm. His jaws close, but not completely, as they would when he makes a kill.

The balance of power

Male cats are more powerful than their partners, and the same is true of most male mammals. A male red deer is up to 50 per cent heavier than the female, or hind, while a male elephant seal can be four times heavier than its partners – something that puts the females in serious danger of getting crushed. But in the case of insects and spiders, the female often has the size advantage, so the balance of power is the other way around.

Male spiders are instinctively wary of their partners, which is just as well because the females can be ten times their size. As a male spider approaches a female, he gives off special coded signals to show that he is a suitor – not simply a meal. In species that have good eyesight, the male waves body parts that look like a pair of tiny arms. Each species has its own pattern of waves, and the closer the male gets, the more energetic his waving becomes.

Web-building spiders have poor eyesight, so they use a different communication system. As the male approaches his gargantuan partner, he gives a series of sharp tugs on her web. If all goes well, this temporarily switches off the

> **Male spiders are instinctively wary of their partners, which is just as well because the females can be ten times their size. As a male spider approaches a female, he gives off special coded signals to show that he is a suitor – not simply a meal.**

female's feeding instincts, allowing the male to come close enough to mate. After mating, he must make a quick departure before the female's predatory instinct switches back on.

Distant partners

For lone hunters, such as leopards, life as a pair rarely lasts long. Once a male leopard has mated successfully, he leaves his partner and their paths may never cross again. Lots of animals – particularly those that live in water – have much more distant relations with the opposite sex than do leopards. Some do not actually touch their partners during mating, while others never even meet. The male crested newt belongs in the first category. He carries out a complicated dance around the female, at the bottom of a pond. The movements are crucial, and if he performs them correctly the female's breeding instincts make her respond. The male then sheds a package of sperm on the pond bottom, and the female moves into position and takes it up. With that exchange, their brief alliance comes to an end.

Distant though it is, the crested newts' behaviour is intimate compared to the breeding system used by giant clams. These gigantic molluscs can weigh over a quarter of a tonne, and are incapable of moving around. Instead of coming together to mate, they release clouds of sperm and eggs directly into the sea. The sperm fertilise the eggs, which then develop into tiny drifting larvae that eventually settle on the seabed. For this to work, it is vital that all the clams in any one place spawn at the same time. Instinct takes care of this by triggering giant clams to release their spawn at particular times, in response to environmental cues – typically in late afternoon when the Moon is either new or full. The same system is used by reef-building corals, which spawn in their millions after dark.

A DATE WITH DANGER In the rain forest of Costa Rica, a female giant orb-weaver spider looms over a male that has walked onto her web. His life depends on triggering her instinct for breeding, rather than the one for feeding.

FINDING A MATE

HERE ARE MORE THAN A MILLION SPECIES IN THE ANIMAL
INGDOM, WHICH COMPLICATES LIFE WHEN IT IS TIME TO
REED. Would-be parents have to track down a mate not only
f the right sex, but also of the right kind. Instead of searching at random,
any animals use signalling systems to track down potential partners. Evolution has
one to extraordinary lengths to vary signals between species, because the more
milar two species are, the more important it is that their signals do not get confused.

*GHTING-UP TIME As
ght falls, Japanese fireflies
cker in the twilight. These
articular fireflies have to
nd a mate quickly, because
eir adult life lasts just a
w days.*

journeys have no set length, and they sometimes last many weeks. While the male roams, he is so focused on finding a partner that he may not even feed.

Many male spiders follow this roving lifestyle, including the common house spider – an impressive and harmless species that often ends its wanderings by falling into baths. It is also used by the Sydney funnel-web – an Australian species whose bite can be fatal. In late summer and autumn, male funnel-web spiders often wander through gardens in search of females in their burrows, following the scent of the females' chemical attractant, and can accidentally end up in houses and garages. Alarmingly, the males are at their most aggressive and bad-tempered at this time of year.

Charm race

Some male animals show no wandering instincts at all. Instead, they put all their energy into creating a spectacle that catches the female's eye. Because the females choose the males, this

INVITING GESTURE Waving its giant claw, a male fiddler crab tries to attract a mate. The claw's pale colour helps to catch the female's eye.

Firefly mating

Fireflies show how amazingly precise these signals can be. There are many species of these nocturnal insects, all of them inhabiting warm regions of the world, and each makes its own light in special light organs on the underside of the abdomen. After dark, females usually light up in thick vegetation, while their suitors fly overhead. Fireflies can switch their lights on and off, and each species has its own distinctive pattern of flashes.

For example, the pyralis firefly from eastern North America flashes on every 5.5 seconds. After lighting up for exactly 0.3 seconds, the male promptly switches off. Female pyralis fireflies instinctively recognise this pattern and flash back if a male flies past. His large downward-facing eyes spot their signals, and he drops to the ground to mate. If the wrong kind of firefly passes overhead, the females do not respond. The male's light slowly disappears as he carries on with his search.

Most fireflies flash independently, but some tropical species instinctively get in step. Thousands can flash on and off together, creating an extraordinary spectacle that looks like an array of tiny Christmas lights.

Who does the searching?

In many animals – including fireflies – it is the male's job to act as a suitor, actively seeking a mate. This makes good sense, because the female often has to expend much more energy on producing and raising the young. One way that males do this is by staking out a private territory where females can find the food and breeding space they need. If a female likes the look of a territory and its owner, she mates with him and moves in.

Animal territories have invisible boundaries, and they vary enormously in size. A European robin's territory can be as small as a backyard; a tiger's can stretch to a staggering 150 km² – and this is just the area that the tiger actually defends from other males. Its complete home range can be 10 times this size – one of the largest of any land animal on Earth.

The territorial instinct holds sway in a huge variety of animals, from rattlesnakes to Siamese fighting fish. But when it is time to breed, the males of some species behave in exactly the opposite way, by setting off on prospecting trips. These

creates a 'charm race', with each male instinctively striving to outclass its rivals. In mangrove swamps, fiddler crabs show what can happen when this race runs to extremes. The female has two small pincers, which are just the right size for picking up food from the mud. The male has one small pincer and one gigantic one that he often holds upright, like a musician with a fiddle or violin. A claw like this is far too clumsy to use for eating. Instead, the male uses it as a signalling device to wave to females, and for ritual combat with other males.

There are over 60 species of fiddlers, and in some mangrove swamps several kinds live side by side. Instinct helps to avoid mix-ups because each kind of fiddler has its own sequence of waves, just as fireflies have their sequences of flashing lights. If a male fiddler crab loses his giant claw, his sex life does not necessarily come to an end. In time, his small claw grows into a giant claw and one of his legs takes over the small claw's work.

Show offs

Having a giant claw may seem like an enormous handicap, but fiddler crabs are not alone in having an inconvenient display feature. Many male birds – including peacocks and birds of paradise – have extravagant and unwieldy plumage that attracts the opposite sex. Male quetzals, from Central America, have such long tails that they cannot fit inside their nests, which are hollowed out in tree trunks. When the male takes his turn incubating the eggs, he instinctively turns around before he sits down. This leaves his green tail feathers curled up over his back with the tips dangling out of the nest's entrance, where they flutter gently in the wind looking like fern leaves.

Peacocks usually display in the open, but birds of paradise live in dense tropical forests in north-eastern Australia, New Guinea and the Molucca islands of Indonesia, where it is harder to be seen. To attract females, they perform bizarre displays accompanied by strange cries. Some stand bolt upright on a perch and spread out feathers that form a fan, but the emperor bird of paradise leans forwards and then swivels upside down, rustling its plumage like a feathery waterfall. Another species, the magnificent bird of

BEST FOOT FORWARD What does an animal look for in its mate? In the case of the blue-footed booby, the answer is feet of the right colour, and an instinct to show them off during courtship displays.

paradise, shows even more remarkable behaviour. It instinctively plucks away the leaves around its perch; this lets in more light and sunshine, so its finery is shown off to the very best effect.

Male birds do not rely only on plumage to catch a female's eye. Atlantic puffins use their multicoloured beaks, while the blue-footed booby shows off his bright blue feet. Both sexes have blue feet and as well as acting as a species identity badge, boobies use them when they are nesting to incubate their eggs. Boobies breed on remote islands and cliffs, and they get their unflattering name from their tameness, which makes them easy to catch. Albatrosses are also tame, and for the same reason. They breed in inaccessible places, so they have no instinctive fear of land-based predators – including human beings.

Look what I've made

To attract a mate, most male animals turn the spotlight on themselves. But in some unusual and fascinating cases, instinct drives would-be suitors to create a special – and at times elaborate – attraction, which they put on display.

On sandy tropical beaches, this way of winning a partner is used by male ghost crabs. Each male digs a burrow and piles the excavated sand into a neat conical heap. Females can spot these spoil heaps from many metres away, and the bigger the heap, the more impressed a female is likely to be. This signalling system is particularly effective because ghost crabs are usually active at night. Even in faint moonlight the female crabs can see the silhouetted mounds, helping them to home in on prospective mates.

Male weaverbirds are using a similar type of signalling system when they build their nests (see pages 30-31). For females, the nest is the main attraction, rather than the male hanging underneath it and fluttering his wings. Nests are essential for breeding, so it is easy to understand why male weavers make them in the quest for a mate. But in bowerbirds, evolution has taken this instinct to bizarre extremes.

Instead of making nests, male bowerbirds use twigs to build extraordinary structures that have no practical value at all. Known as bowers, most are shaped like narrow, roofless corridors, but the biggest – made by the gardener bowerbird – looks like a thatched cottage and can be over 2 m high. The bower's sole function is to attract females. Once a female has mated, she flies off to make a nest and raise her family entirely on her own.

BOWERBIRD

THE FINEST NUPTIAL CHAMBER IN **THE ANIMAL WORLD IS BUILT BY THE SATIN BOWERBIRD, FROM EASTERN AUSTRALIA.** This elaborate structure – known as an avenue bower – is made of two parallel rows of arching twigs and is up to 50 cm long. The bower is constructed on a mat of sticks, which the male bird spreads out on the forest floor. Despite its complexity, the bower is not a nest. It attracts females, but after the pair have mated, the female leaves the male and his bower and lays her eggs elsewhere.

To increase the appeal of his bower, the male satin bowerbird decorates it with all kinds of objects: his only rule is that they must be yellow or blue. Berries, flowers and feathers are the most popular natural choices, but satin bowerbirds also pick up man-made objects, such as bottle-tops and plastic pen-caps. The male's skills also include painting: using a wad of bark, he daubs the bower with a bluish paint made of plant juices mixed with his saliva. He seems to be almost houseproud in the care he takes with his creation, removing any flowers when they wilt and replacing them with fresh supplies.

When everything is to the male's satisfaction, his physical display begins. He picks up an item from his collection and carries out a peculiar dance. Calling softly, he leaps about on the mat of twigs, and periodically freezes as if he has forgotten what follows. This extraordinary behaviour, in its remarkable setting, acts like a magnet to female satin bowerbirds. The male mates with any females that are attracted by his work, but he plays no part in building a nest or raising the young.

VITAL STATISTICS

CLASS: Aves
ORDER: Passeriformes
SPECIES: *Ptilonorhynchus violaceus*
HABITAT: Tropical forest
DISTRIBUTION: Eastern Australia
KEY FEATURES: Master builder of the bird world, creating elaborate bower used to attract and court females

SIGNALLING WITH SOUND

TO HUMAN EARS, A FROG'S CROAK OR THE TRILL OF A GRASSHOPPER IS JUST ANOTHER SOUND. But to the animals that make them, sounds convey vital information in the quest for a mate. Like musicians in an orchestra, animals produce sounds in many different ways. Some play alone, but others set up a deafening chorus that can be louder than a performance in a concert hall.

Grasshoppers and their relatives are experts at this way of attracting partners. Per gram of body weight, they are among the noisiest animals in the world. Male mole crickets, which live underground, produce some of the loudest calls by creating their own amplifiers – Y-shaped burrows with two entrance tunnels that flare outwards like tiny trumpets. When a mole cricket calls from the junction of the Y, his call can be heard up to 1 km away. Other cricket species are ventriloquists – they use sound frequencies that make it difficult for predators to pinpoint where they are.

Unlike mammals and birds, crickets and grasshoppers make sound mechanically by scraping body parts together, a technique called stridulation. Crickets rub their wings together; grasshoppers rub their legs against their hindwings. Each species has a different call, which the males play over and over again. Females instinctively respond to the 'right' call, heading towards it even if it is a recording played back in a cage. For small animals like these, sound is an ideal way to attract mates, because it works well in overgrown habitats and is just as effective at night as by day.

MESSAGES IN THE GRASS Rubbing his hindlegs against his body, a male grasshopper broadcasts his distinctive call sign in a summer meadow. In warm weather, he sings for many hours each day.

SUBMARINE SINGERS Humpback whales may be able to communicate further than any other animals on Earth. By listening to a male's song, a female can find out lots about him before the pair eventually meet.

Songs in the sea

The deep oceans are far from silent. Many fish communicate by squeaks and grunts, which they make by squeezing their swimbladders – a kind of internal, gas-filled float. Humpback whales do something infinitely more impressive – they sing haunting, mournful and strangely moving songs. These caused a sensation when first discovered by scientists in the early 1970s and became a bestselling item in record shops worldwide.

More is now known about humpback songs, although many questions still remain. The songs are produced during the breeding season, and only by the males. This makes it likely that they are used to attract females or to keep rival males away. But the songs' structure is still unexplained. A single song can last for up to 20 minutes, with a complex sequence of separate phrases, and a singing whale may repeat its song for hours at a time. Furthermore, the song has regional variations. Pacific humpbacks sing a different version to Atlantic ones; and in both, the song gradually changes over time. One thing is certain: because sound carries over enormous distances in water, humpbacks' songs allowe them to stay in contact even if they are separated by hundreds of kilometres of sea.

Learning to sing

Relatively few mammals use sound to attract a mate, but song is a crucial way for birds to get in touch. Although some birds, such as parrots and starlings, are gifted mimics and can copy all kinds of sounds, many species have such characteristic songs that they can be identified by their song alone.

Research with young birds has shown that in most cases songs are partly inherited, partly learned. If a young finch never hears adults singing, it will still sing when it grows up, showing that instinct is at work, but its song will be much simpler than a wild finch's, with far fewer individual notes. This is because young birds inherit the basics; they learn the finer points from the older birds around them. This learning stage explains why many birds develop 'regional dialects' – a feature they share with humpback whales and ourselves.

FACTS

MALE CICADAS GENERATE THE LOUDEST CHORUSES IN the insect world. At a distance of 18 m, the sound produced by cicadas in a single tree can measure up to 100 decibels – louder than a pneumatic drill. Cicadas generate sounds by clicking membranes that snap in and out like the lid of a can.

IN JUST ONE HOUR the brown thrasher – a North American bird – can produce over 2400 separate bursts of song.

THE SNAPPING SHRIMP produces one of the loudest non-vocal calls in the sea. By snapping one of its claws shut, it creates a bubble of water that collapses, sending out a shock wave.

FACTS

INFLATED FOR SOUND For tiny creatures about 6 cm long, male red-eyed treefrogs from eastern Australia can create a deafening chorus on summer nights as they attract females to rain-filled pools. Each call consists of a series of 'aaark' sounds, ending with a trill or chirp.

SIGNALLING WITH SCENT

THE MOMENT A MALE GRASSHOPPER STOPS SINGING, IT LOSES ALMOST ALL ITS SEX APPEAL. Animals that signal by smell, in contrast, leave a scent that can linger for days. This way of getting in touch relies entirely on instinct. Animals use a range of distinctive chemicals, called pheromones, to get their messages across and unlike a sound signal, a scent signal cannot be modulated to mean different things.

With their nocturnal lifestyle, moths rely almost entirely on scent to find a mate. Female emperor moths give off a pheromone that the males detect using their feathery antennae. The sensitivity

SWEEP NET Each of the male emperor moth's antennae has over 30 cm of fine filaments, helping it to collect scent molecules in the air.

of these antennae almost defies belief. They can detect individual molecules of the pheromone, allowing males to track down females as far as 10 km away. Vapourer moths use a similar system, but in their case the female is wingless, so cannot fly. She releases pheromones from her hiding place, and the male moth flies 'upstream' until he tracks her down. Male cinnabar moths are not so patient. Drawn by pheromones, they often gather around female chrysalises, ready to mate as soon as the females emerge.

Scent signalling evolved at the very dawn of animal life, long before animals had eyes, ears or well-developed brains. This explains why it works purely by instinct, and why it is so widespread. Many marine worms, snails and crustaceans use scent to find their mates, and so do freshwater animals that live in caves. Scent signals can be useful in other ways as well – for example, when a young barnacle comes to the end of its time as a floating larva and becomes an adult fastened to a rock. Like a lunar landing, this touchdown is a critical moment. Once it comes in to land, the barnacle is committed; it cannot change its mind or reposition itself. To select a suitable site, it scans the water for the scent of adult barnacles. When it detects these chemicals, it promptly settles down alongside. This instinctive guidance system means that barnacles attract each other. In the choicest locations, over 10,000 can be crammed into each square metre of rocky shore.

Chemicals in the air

Animals have many different ways of sensing chemical scents. Some detect them with their skin, with their antennae or even with their feet. We pick up airborne scents with our noses, but many vertebrates also have chemical-sensitive nerve endings in the roof of their mouths. Called Jacobson's organ, this mechanism is particularly well developed in snakes. To smell the air, a snake first flicks out its tongue. It then presses the tongue against the roof of its mouth, which transfers the scent molecules to the nerve endings that can identify them.

Humans do not have a Jacobson's organ, but many other mammals do. In hoofed mammals, such as horses and buffalo, it plays a key part in the scent signalling system that helps males to find a mate. When a female is ready to mate, she gives off pheromones in her urine. Attracted by her pheromones, males pursue her relentlessly, and fights often break out as rivals try to assert their right to mate.

TESTING THE AIR Curling back his upper lip, a male Cape buffalo exposes his Jacobson's organ to the air. This instinctive behaviour – called flehmen – is displayed by many hoofed mammals during the breeding season.

COURTSHIP RITUALS

ONCE TWO FUTURE PARTNERS HAVE COME TOGETHER, INSTINCT LAUNCHES A CRITICAL STAGE OF THE REPRODUCTIVE PROCESS. Not only does aggression have to be defused – the pair also has to work together as a team. This is often achieved through courtship dances and other rituals that instinct triggers and controls. At its briefest, courtship lasts just long enough for the male to mate and go on his way. But in animals that share parenting – including many mammals and birds – courtship can last for days and create a partnership that may last for life.

GIVING A GIFT Clinging to a leaf by his front legs, a male dance fly mates with a female, while she is busy feeding on an insect that he has just given her.

Courtship gifts

For male dance flies, courtship gets off to an unusual start. Before the male seeks out a female, he searches for prey. When he has caught a small insect, he wraps it in a silken shroud and slings the package beneath his legs. Female dance flies, like female spiders, are aggressive; before they will mate, they need to be appeased. This is where the male's gift-wrapped package comes into play. Hovering in midair, he passes her his courtship gift, and then pairs with her while she is disentangling the silk wrapping. By the time the female has unwrapped and eaten her present, the male has finished mating and left the scene. The female lays her eggs some time later, and her young grow up on their own.

This intriguing game of pass-the-parcel is just one variant in the dance fly repertoire. Some male dance flies do not offer the females a gift, and may pay the price with their lives. In other species, the tables are turned. The male offers a gift, but when the female unwraps it, she discovers that there is nothing inside.

Stepping out

Insects, and most land animals, use internal fertilisation: the male physically pairs up with his partner so that he can introduce his sperm directly into her body. Scorpions use a different technique, similar to that used by newts underwater. The male produces sperm in a sealed packet called a spermatophore. He then guides the female over it, so that it is picked up by her reproductive tract.

This way of mating requires a special kind of courtship, because the male scorpion has to steer the female into place. To do this, he grasps her by her pincers – a position that keeps him safely away from her sting. The two scorpions then embark on a zigzagging dance, which can last for several hours. Once courtship and mating are over, instinct makes the couple disengage. The male promptly abandons his former mate, but she has many weeks of parenting ahead. Instead of laying eggs, she gives birth to live young and carries them about on her back.

Suitors in waiting

In mammals, courtship often seems to get off to a difficult start, with the female trying to fend off the male. Zebra stallions risk a well-aimed kick, while male lions risk being slashed by the female's claws. This behaviour looks alarming, but it is actually

LOVERS IN ARMS During their elaborate courtship dance, two African fat-tailed scorpions keep their pincers firmly locked, so that neither can sting the other.

COURTSHIP KISS Nuzzling his mate, a male giraffe also keeps an eye out for other males. A stronger rival could try to intervene before he has a chance to mate.

part of normal courtship procedure. Female mammals are often receptive for just a short period of time, when their egg cells are ready to be fertilised. They attract males before they can mate, but until the right moment arrives, all the male can do is to stay close and wait. In hoofed mammals, such as giraffes, this waiting period can last for several days. The male doggedly follows his partner, and does his best to keep rival males away. From time to time he nudges her with his muzzle, but she instinctively pulls away. Finally, the female becomes receptive and her behaviour abruptly changes. Instead of walking away, she stands still and allows the male to mate.

Mammal courtship hardly ever features complex dances because many of their courtship signals are carried by smell. In birds, things are very different. Birds have a poor sense of smell, but keen eyesight, so for them visual displays are a key part of pairing up. Many males show off their plumage, and some put on special display flights to impress potential mates. Bird courtship also often involves exchanging food or nesting material – something that happens in the dramatic midair courtship of buzzards and the waterborne dances of grebes (see page 64).

Free-for-all

Because the instinct to mate and pass on genes is so strong, animal courtship can trigger off intense competition in males trying to find a partner. In some animals, such as the common toad, males outnumber females, and an unruly scrabble can break out as males struggle to win the same mate. Male toads have a powerful clasping instinct, which makes them grip the female's waist. A female in her breeding pond can find herself loaded up with six or more suitors, all clinging on tightly as she struggles to move. The males kick and push to dislodge their rivals, and by the time the female is ready to spawn, normally just one male is left.

In the case of North American garter snakes, the free-for-all is even more intense. In cold regions, garter snakes hibernate underground in winter and mate when they emerge in spring. Females are larger than males, and they give off a pheromone that draws males towards them. The effect is spectacular – and nightmarish for anyone who is frightened of snakes. A handful of females can be surrounded by hundreds of males, creating a writhing 'mating ball'.

ANATOMY OF A DANCE

GREBES CARRY OUT SOME OF THE MOST COMPLEX AND GRACEFUL COURTSHIP RITUALS IN THE ANIMAL WORLD. Their elaborate dances are made up of several separate stages and show how instinct cements a bond between two birds. Clumsy on land and slow to get airborne, grebes are in their true element on water. Thanks to their air-filled plumage, they float almost as well as corks, but they can disappear with barely a ripple when they dive. Unlike ducks, grebes' legs are set far back along their bodies, and they have spreading lobes on each of their toes. This unusual anatomy allows them to tread water almost vertically – a talent they show off during the crescendo of their display, known as the 'penguin dance'. Another special feature of grebe dances is that the female is almost as energetic as the male. Instead of displaying alone, grebes court like a pair of ballet dancers carrying out a pas de deux.

Step by step

Grebe dances usually open with the male approaching the female in a 'discovery ceremony', and inviting her to respond. In great crested grebes, the male holds his head high, with his decorative crest and ruffs fully spread. As he nears the female, he hunches

FACE TO FACE At the climax of the 'penguin dance' sequence in their courtship, two great crested grebes present each other with weed they have collected from the bottom of the lake.

A grebe that performs the 'wrong' steps is likely to be from the wrong species. By sticking strictly to the rules of their dance, grebes ensure that they have found a mate that belongs to the same species as themselves.

down and opens his wings, waiting for her to react. At this point, the female stands up straight and treads water, before settling down again to face the male. Suddenly, the dance changes gear: the two birds face each other and wag their beaks up and down. Sometimes this ritual tails off, but at the height of their courtship they begin the penguin dance.

The penguin dance starts with both birds upending and disappearing below the surface. The two dive down to the bottom of their pond or lake, where they snatch up pieces of weed in their beaks. Returning to the surface, they position themselves face to face and suddenly rear up by paddling furiously with their legs. At the same time they present each other with the weed, wagging their heads from side to side.

The dance concludes as dramatically as it begins, as one of the birds patters across the water in a retreat ceremony. In some grebes, two birds rear upright and speed across the surface side by side, like a pair of waterskiers being pulled by an invisible boat. This spectacular display – called rushing – can be performed by a mixed pair or by two rival males.

SIDE BY SIDE Two western grebes speed across a lake in North America. This 'rushing' display is a family feature in many species of grebe in different parts of the world.

What does it mean?

By studying grebe dances, scientists have pieced together the origins of this bizarre behaviour. One thing is certain: grebes did not suddenly 'invent' their dances at some moment in the distant past. Instead, like all courtship displays, its movements evolved from pieces of existing behaviour. Over countless generations, these were slowly adapted or ritualised, so that they became ways of signalling to an existing partner or a potential mate.

Some of the grebes' dance movements are ritualised versions of take-off behaviour – a slow process in grebes because they have small wings. The penguin dance may have evolved from courtship feeding, a type of behaviour that is seen in many birds, when the male offers the female food. Courtship feeding is itself a ritual, and almost certainly evolved from the powerful instinct that drives parent birds to feed their young. In courting robins, for example, the female opens her wings and begs for food, just like a young bird would in the nest. Unlike dancing, this ritual has the practical function of ensuring that the female is well fed before she starts to lay her eggs.

Strictly ballroom

Unlike human dancers, courting grebes cannot improvise when they carry out a display. They have to perform all the movements in the correct way and in the correct order, or their partner will fail to respond and the dance will come to a halt. If this happens often enough, the whole process of courtship stalls and the two grebes slowly drift apart. This might seem unnecessarily fussy, but it has evolved for a good reason. A grebe that performs the 'wrong' steps is likely to be from the wrong species. By sticking strictly to the rules of their dance, grebes ensure that they have found a mate that belongs to the same species as themselves.

WHO DOES THE DANCING?

Bird courtship displays are closely linked to differences in the way different species breed. Some have just one partner during their lives, which makes it important that they form a lasting bond. Others have several partners, without forming long-term bonds.

TYPE OF PARTNERSHIP	COURTSHIP DISPLAY	EXAMPLES
Each male mates with one female. Partnership often lasts for life.	Both birds display	Gannets Grebes Penguins
Each male mates with several females in a breeding season.	Male displays to females	Bowerbirds Peacocks
Each female mates with several males during a breeding season.	Female displays to males	Jacanas Phalaropes

TESTS OF STRENGTH

ON A SCOTTISH HILLSIDE, TWO RED DEER STAGS CLASH DURING THEIR ANNUAL RUT. The victor will win the right to breed and the chance to pass on his genes. The fight is vicious, and stags' antlers are lethally sharp, but instinct ensures that the contest is played to strict rules. Throughout the animal world, males fight each other for the right to mate. Crabs battle with their claws, and rhinoceroses joust with their horns. Stag beetles grapple each other with their hornlike jaws, sometimes lifting up their opponent and dashing it to the ground. These confrontations look dramatic, and in some species – such as elephant seals – they can end in severe injury or even death. But in most, instinct provides ways of deciding the winner before any real damage is done.

POWER STRUGGLE Pushing with all their strength, two male red deer struggle for supremacy during the annual rutting season. After the rut ends, they shed their antlers and grow a new pair, usually larger than the previous pair.

Winner takes all

Red deer fights begin when one stag challenges another for control of his harem of females, or hinds. The intruder throws down the gauntlet by bellowing, and the defender replies in kind. This is the first cutoff point: if the intruder is out-bellowed, it instinctively backs away. If not, the contest continues. The two stags approach each other, and then walk up and down with their bodies side by side. Again, the intruder may abandon his challenge at this point. But if he persists, the two stags face each other, lock antlers and attempt to push each other backwards. This push-of-war can last for many minutes, until one stag weakens and finds itself forced into reverse. It disengages its antlers, and then suffers the humiliation of having to run away.

By fighting, a stag demonstrates his health and vigour, and his suitability as a partner. If he is successful, he may mate with over a dozen females during the course of the rutting season, and he may repeat this success for several years. But the rut uses up huge amounts of energy, and age takes its toll. Eventually, a younger stag will beat him in battle and his breeding days will come to an ignominious end.

Courtship arenas

Medieval knights on horseback fought in jousts, where they could show off to best effect. In a remarkable parallel, the males of some bird species joust at traditional courtship arenas known as leks. This behaviour is common in ground-nesting gamebirds, such as sage grouse, and the spectacle is watched keenly by the females, which visit the lek to choose a mate.

For sage grouse, lekking is a serious business, but to human onlookers it can have a distinctly comic appearance. The males do not come to blows; instead, they strut about self-importantly with their wings spread and tails fanned. At the same time, they show off their prowess by inflating a pair of neck sacs, which reach down almost to the ground. These sacs periodically deflate with a loud pop, which can be heard some distance away. The dominant male is the one who manages to occupy the centre of the lek, forcing the other males towards the edges. Female birds are instinctively attracted to him, and he will father the most young.

A handful of species, including the northern jacana, or lilytrotter, reverse the roles in their courtship contests. The female jacana is highly aggressive and fights other females to claim a male. A successful female can have up to four mates, each sitting on a separate nest, brooding a separate clutch of her eggs. The female defends her territory, and leaves her partners to raise her young.

MATING

Female mantises have an unfortunate habit of treating their partners as prey. Without warning, the female may twist around and eat the male, starting with his head.

THE URGE TO MATE IS ONE OF THE MOST POWERFUL INSTINCTS IN NATURE: IT HAS TO BE, BECAUSE WITHOUT IT, SPECIES WOULD NOT SURVIVE. Mating itself takes many forms: it can last for seconds or for hours, and can take place on land, in water or in the air. Mating ensures that the female's egg cells are fertilised so that they can start developing into young.

For large land mammals, such as elephants and rhinos, mating can be a challenge – elephants often need several attempts to make it work. As he rises up unsteadily on his hind legs, a mature bull – who can weigh up to 5 tonnes – puts a colossal strain on his partner and on himself. In comparison, rhinos seem almost nimble. Once the male rhino is in position, the female instinctively stands still; and she manages to support her partner's weight for up to half an hour.

Sea mammals do not have these weight problems because the water buoys them up. However, pairing is not easy for animals without legs or feet. Unlike most land mammals, whales and dolphins mate face-to-face, although they sometimes end up head to tail. Little is known about the mating habits of the largest whales, even though many species – such as the grey whale and humpback – gather close to land in traditional mating grounds when the time comes to breed.

Partners in the air

Insects are the only animals that routinely mate on the wing, and even they often start by pairing on the ground. Mating butterflies sometimes fly back to back, with the larger female towing the smaller male. With dragonflies, the flying formation is the other way around. The male dragonfly has claspers at the end of his abdomen, which he uses to grip the female behind the back of the head. Once they are airborne, the male steers the tandem over water so that his partner can scatter her eggs.

In birds, mating often involves a delicate balancing act, and almost always happens with the female either on the ground or clinging to a perch. Just one bird, the common swift, sometimes manages the remarkable feat of mating in midair.

Strange encounters

Mating is an intimate procedure, but this does not mean that the partners instinctively treat each other with respect. The male bedbug has a particularly alarming mating technique that involves using his sex organs to punch a hole in his partner's side. He injects his sperm through the hole and into her blood, and this eventually carries it to her eggs. Fortunately for the female, the wound soon heals and she is none the worse for the experience.

In deep-sea angler fish, mating is even more bizarre. Females can be bigger than a football, while the males are often less than 2 cm long. Unlike the female, the male does not have teeth and cannot feed. His survival depends on finding a mate, who he tracks down using his keen sense of smell. When he locates a female, he hooks onto her flesh using small spines on his snout. In time, his mouth fuses with her body, so that he becomes permanently attached, like a parasite. The female provides him with food from her bloodstream, and in return he fertilises her eggs.

UNDERWATER EMBRACE Two Atlantic spotted dolphins mate in the sea off the Bahamas. The male is larger than his partner, and he courts her by swimming around her in tight circles, nuzzling her with his beak and clicking loudly.

Death on duty

Most mammals and birds mate several times during their lives. But in simpler animals, such as insects, the females often mate just once. Their instincts drive them to choose the most suitable partner, while the males' instincts spur them to mate with as many females as they can.

These differences are highlighted in spectacular fashion by praying mantises. The female is larger than the male, and she feeds voraciously to produce her clutch of eggs. The male approaches her cautiously, moving into position from behind. If all goes well, he detaches himself after mating and makes his escape to mate with other females as the breeding season goes on. But female mantises have a habit of treating their partners as prey. Without warning, the female may twist around so that she can eat the male, starting with his head. Even when he is headless his nervous system still functions, and mating continues while the female completes her meal. When she has eaten all she can reach, what is left of the male's body drops to the ground.

Death during mating is a macabre and rare event. Even in mantises, it is the exception rather than the rule. But the male's sacrifice is not in vain, because by being eaten by the female he helps to feed his young. Males are not alone in sacrificing themselves in this way. In some spider species the female dies while she is incubating her eggs, and the young spiderlings feed on her body after they hatch. In the case of Pacific salmon, such as the sockeye and the chinook, both parents die after they have spawned. Their bodies break down and fertilise the water, helping to give the young salmon a good start in life when they eventually hatch from their eggs.

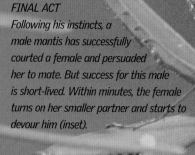

FINAL ACT
Following his instincts, a male mantis has successfully courted a female and persuaded her to mate. But success for this male is short-lived. Within minutes, the female turns on her smaller partner and starts to devour him (inset).

START

ING
OUT

4

HEADING TOWARDS THE WATERS OF THE SOUTHERN OCEAN, A FEMALE HUMPBACK WHALE GENTLY NUZZLES HER 2 TONNE CALF. Instinct makes her fiercely protective of her young charge – vital behaviour for an animal that has a family of just one. Gradually, instinct will also loosen her attachment so that the calf can gain its independence and become a parent itself. This kind of maternal protection has a deep resonance for us, because instinct makes human parents behave in similar ways. In the animal world as a whole, close bonds between parents and offspring are the exception rather than the rule. Some parents are attentive, while many take little or no interest in their young. For those prompted by instinct to be careful parents, the investment they make in time and energy pays off by giving their generally fewer young the best chance of survival.

APPROACHES TO
PARENTING

WHEN YOUNG TURTLES HATCH ON OPEN BEACHES, PARENTS ARE NOT ON HAND TO GUIDE THEM DOWN TO THE SEA or to protect them as they go. Life starts with a dangerous race past hungry predators towards the safety of the waves. Instinct ensures that young turtles know which way to go, but otherwise they are on their own.

Compared to some creatures, turtles have a perilous start in life, but they are not unique in this. A huge variety of animals – including almost all invertebrate species – start life on their own. Without parents around to protect them, the majority of these young animals soon die, but nature balances the books by producing them in mind-boggling numbers. Female turtles lay up to 100 eggs in each nest, and some species dig up to six nests in a year. Common frogs are even more productive, laying several thousand eggs when they spawn. Even they pale in comparison to ocean sunfish, which lay up to 300 million eggs each time they breed. Weighing up to 2 tonnes each, these incredibly prolific but lethargic fish show no parental instincts at all.

RUNNING THE GAUNTLET On a beach in Costa Rica, young turtles scrabble out of the nest and head for the sea. Instinct prompts all the baby turtles in the nest to break cover at the same time, making it harder for predators to pick them off one by one.

THE ADDER FAMILY A female adder gives birth to up to 15 live young, but only breeds every two or three years. For their first few days, the young snakes stay by her side.

WHO CARES?

UNLIKE TURTLES OR SUNFISH, SOME PARENTS INHERIT A STRONG INSTINCT TO STAY WITH THEIR YOUNG. All mammals are like this, and so are the overwhelming majority of birds. The rare exceptions include a group of strange gamebirds – the megapodes, or mound-builders, from Australia and South-east Asia. Instead of building nests, megapodes incubate their young in 'compost heaps', which they make by scraping together sand and leaves. These mounds can be up to 2 m high and 6 m across, and the rotting vegetation produces its own warmth. The parents lay their eggs in the mound and then stay nearby, adjusting the temperature by adding more leaves or sand. When the eggs hatch, the young scramble out of the mound unaided and immediately take up life on their own. They are the only young birds that can fly as soon as they hatch.

Compared to mammals and birds, caring parents are much less common in the rest of the animal world, although some snakes and amphibians look after their young, as do many fish, spiders and bugs. Even so, being a 'caring' parent can mean many different things. Chimps look after their young for up to five years, while spiders often lose interest soon after their young's first moult, which usually takes place a few days after the young break out of their eggs.

FAST AND SLOW BREEDERS

Large mammals breed more slowly than small ones. House mice can produce over 30 generations in the time it takes an African elephant to grow up.

SPECIES	AVERAGE NUMBER OF OFFSPRING
House mouse	60 a year
Virginia opossum	40 a year
Red fox	5 a year
Kangaroo	1 a year
Humpback whale	1 every 2 years
Chimpanzee	1 every 3 years
African elephant	1 every 5 years

Mine, not yours

When African dogs return from a hunt, the adults join forces to feed the pack's young. A young pup may be suckled by three or four females, including its mother. When it starts to eat solid food, any of the adults will feed it pieces of meat, and this carries on until the pup is 10 weeks old, when it begins to feed itself. This kind of behaviour is very unusual. Most animals care for their own young, but their parental instincts end there.

For young seabirds, extreme favouritism by adults can have deadly results. If a young tern wanders away from its mother, it can expect no help from other adults, even if it is attacked by a predator. Worse still, other adult terns may attack it themselves. Far from triggering protective instincts in adults, an 'alien' youngster triggers their instinct to defend their nests. An even worse fate lies in store for lion cubs if their pride is taken over by a group of intruding males. Once the new males have assumed control, instinct drives them to seek out all the cubs and kill them. Why do some animals behave in this way? Because it is built into their genes. Instincts have evolved to help animals survive, giving them the best chance of breeding and passing on their genes. There is no survival value in helping someone else's young, which is why male lions kill existing cubs. The main exception to this rule is when the adults in a group are close relatives, as they are in an elephant herd or a pack of African dogs. Here, helping any of the young does pay as all the young share some genes with every adult.

PROTECTIVE PARENTS

PARENTAL CARE OFTEN STARTS LONG BEFORE THE YOUNG EMERGE INTO THE OUTSIDE WORLD. Mammals nourish their young inside their bodies, or in the safety of a pouch, while birds settle down to incubate their eggs. Incubation looks uneventful, but it is a complex operation, and instinct controls every detail. Some birds start incubating when their first egg has been laid, but most wait until they have laid a complete clutch, so that the nestlings all hatch at the same time. Birds cannot count their eggs, so instinct tells them when to stop laying and when to start sitting on the nest. Another instinct makes them turn the eggs so that they are evenly warmed. In species where only the female incubates, instinct makes her sit tight; if both parents incubate, instinct releases the sitting bird at change-over time.

Birds can show a great passion for incubation, but they are not necessarily good at recognising their own eggs. With a little prompting, some will brood all kinds of egg-shaped objects, from pieces of fruit to plastic balls. If a bird's eggs are removed, instinct often makes her lay more. The record for a mallard duck is an amazing 146 eggs, instead of the normal 12.

Early days

When eggs hatch, different parental behaviour is triggered. Many songbirds carry off the empty shells so they cannot fall to the ground and give away the location of the nest to predators.

MISPLACED DEVOTION Driven by its parental instincts, a Hawaiian albatross tries to incubate an egg-shaped fishing buoy, while its partner looks on.

Once this is done, and the chicks start begging, the parents' instinct sends them off to find food. Ground-nesting birds react differently because their young are better developed when they hatch and can collect food for themselves. Female gamebirds, such as partridges and quail, lead their chicks away from the nest. As the family sets off they keep in touch by sound, with the mother bird calling insistently to any chicks that go astray.

Like most reptiles, crocodiles do not incubate their eggs; instead, they bury them in the ground. But for them as well, sound is an important trigger for the mother's instincts. Just before baby crocodiles hatch they make a yelping noise, and the mother responds by gently digging them up. Once the eggs are exposed, she sometimes tears open their leathery shells to help the young emerge, before picking them up in her jaws and carrying them to the water's edge.

For young marsupials, the start of life involves an even more hazardous journey. Even the biggest, the red kangaroo, gives birth to tiny young, just 2.5 cm long and weighing less than a sugar-cube. At this stage, a joey has no fur and its eyes are not fully formed. Only its front legs

GENTLE JAWS Perched in its mother's mouth, a young crocodile gets a safe ride from the nest to the water's edge.

SAFETY IN A POUCH Kangaroos give birth to just one young, or joey, at a time, so it has its mother's pouch to itself as it grows. At moments of danger the pouch tightens up, holding the joey firmly inside.

function, and it uses these to climb from the mother's reproductive tract to the safety of her pouch. Once inside, it fastens onto her nipple, and the nipple swells so that the joey is stuck fast. The joey stays in the pouch for four months before making its first excursions.

Compared to some other marsupials, the joey's childhood seems pampered, despite its difficult start. Virginia opossums typically give birth to 20 young twice a year. The mother does not have a true pouch – the young hang from her teats like pieces of fruit as she climbs about in trees. To make matters tougher, she has only about a dozen teats and it is rare for all of them to work. Only young lucky enough to latch onto a functioning teat survive.

Role reversal

In a typical animal family, the female raises the young on her own, but in a small number of species the caring instinct is much stronger in the male. One of the most widespread examples of this is found in predatory freshwater bugs. The female glues her eggs to the male's hindwings; struggling to swim and unable to fly, he carries them until they hatch.

Male midwife toads, from Europe, take a more pro-active approach. The male gathers up the strings of eggs produced by his partner and wraps them around his legs to protect them from predators. Several weeks later, when the eggs are ready to hatch, he lowers his legs into a pond so that the tadpoles can hatch into

BACKPACKING BUG A male giant water bug with eggs fastened to its hindwings.

water. Caring fathers are also common among fish. Jawfish and cichlids incubate their partners' eggs in their mouths, while male seahorses use a special pouch, which gives them a pregnant look.

Among birds, male-only brooders form a distinctive club: they include ostriches, emus, cassowaries and kiwis, as well as a scattering of species in which each female mates with several males, such as the red phalarope. But for sheer perseverance in the task, nothing beats the male emperor penguin, which incubates a single egg throughout the dark Antarctic winter in some of the coldest conditions anywhere on Earth.

OPEN WIDE Instinct stops a male jawfish swallowing while he protects his partner's eggs.

LARGEST OF THE WORLD'S PENGUINS,

THE EMPEROR IS ALSO THE ONLY ONE THAT INCUBATES ITS EGGS ON ICE. EMPERORS START THEIR COURTSHIP IN MAY – LATE AUTUMN IN ANTARCTICA – AND THE FEMALE LAYS HER SINGLE EGG WHEN THE DAYS ARE LESS THAN FOUR HOURS LONG. The male immediately takes charge of the egg, cradling it on his feet, while the female sets off across the ice towards the ocean, where she spends the winter feeding. As winter darkness sets in and the air temperature drops to –40°C, the male emperors huddle together for warmth. Despite the bitter cold, the male penguins keep the eggs at a temperature of 34°C, thanks to a flap of skin that covers the egg and holds it close to the penguin's body. In emperor penguins, incubation lasts for seven weeks, during which time the males cannot feed. By the time the egg hatches, each male has lost over a third of his body weight. But relief is at hand. As the Sun reappears, the females return, walking and tobogganing across the ice. They take charge of the chicks, while the males head out to sea to feed after their winter fast. This extraordinary breeding system ensures that emperor chicks are fully grown by midsummer, giving them time to feed up before the next winter begins.

VITAL STATISTICS

CLASS: Aves

ORDER: Sphenisciformes

FAMILY: *Aptenodytes forsteri*

HABITAT: Cold seas and polar ice

DISTRIBUTION: Antarctica and Southern Ocean

KEY FEATURES: Largest penguin, up to 1.1 m tall; the only bird that breeds on ice, and that never sets foot on land

EMPEROR
PENGUIN

NATURE'S POWERS

CANNIBALISM

SOME ANIMAL PARENTS CAN BE WORSE THAN UNCARING. Adult Komodo dragons live on the ground, but their young live in trees – a wise precaution as their parents have a cannibalistic streak. Komodos are the world's largest lizards, with appetites to match. Instinct tells juveniles not to linger on the ground once they have hatched. True cannibalism is rare in animals because most predators instinctively avoid eating their own kind, but there are exceptions. Insects and spiders sometimes dine on their mates, and adult Komodo dragons occasionally manage to catch youngsters that venture within reach. And for some animals – including certain species of butterflies, birds and sharks – cannibalism is a normal part of growing up.

Cain and Abel
Orange-tip butterflies lay their eggs singly, one to a plant, instinctively spacing them out so that each caterpillar will have enough to eat. But if food plants are hard to find, the female butterfly may be forced to lay several eggs on each plant. When this happens, cannibalism thins the ranks once the caterpillars have hatched out. Each

BRIEF LIFE An adult great green bushcricket eats a young one of the same species.

time two caterpillars meet, the stronger of the two grasps the other with its front legs and starts feeding on its flesh. Eventually, just one caterpillar is left.

Some birds hatch with a murderous instinct that puts their siblings at risk. Sometimes known as 'cainism' – after the biblical brothers Cain and Abel – it is most common in boobies, owls and birds of prey. Eagles and buzzards often lay only two eggs, a few days apart, which also hatch a few days apart. It is not unusual for the first chick to eat its younger, smaller nestmate while its parents are away looking for food. Young owls can be just as aggressive. One long-term study of barn-owl nests found that two-thirds of the deaths among chicks involved one eating another. This grisly behaviour is far removed from the cosy cartoon world of animal families, but animals start life with an overriding instinct to stay alive. By providing food, the victims of cannibalism help their bigger siblings to survive.

Cannibalism before birth

The strangest kind of cannibalism occurs in sandtiger sharks, a species found in warm coastal waters throughout the world and often kept in marine aquariums. Instead of laying eggs, as many sharks do, female sandtigers give birth to live young. The female has two separate uteruses, and early in her pregnancy each uterus contains about a dozen embryos at different stages of development. For young sandtigers this is when survival of the fittest begins, as the oldest embryo in each uterus sets about eating all the others, until it is the only one left. By the time the mother gives birth, her two well-fed offspring can measure nearly 1 m long, which is almost half as long as she is. Although her family numbers just two, the young sharks' size gives them a very good chance of survival.

PARENTS ON THE PROWL Young Komodo dragons have light bodies and are good at climbing trees. They need to be – particularly when a 3 m long cannibalistic adult lumbers into view.

FAMILY TIES

IN ANY FAMILY, IT IS VITAL THAT PARENTS AND YOUNG CAN RECOGNISE EACH OTHER. Young animals 'lock on' to their parents by a special kind of learning called imprinting, which operates during the first few days.

Imprinting was discovered in the 1930s by Austrian zoologist Konrad Lorenz – a pioneer of the study of animal behaviour. In a famous series of experiments, he found that goslings imprint on the first moving object they see after hatching, which is normally an adult goose. By brooding goslings in an incubator and being present when they hatched, Lorenz found that the goslings would imprint on him. Wherever Lorenz went, the goslings followed.

Unlike most learning, imprinting is instinctive and happens only for a short period in early life. Goslings imprint on their parents during their first 24 hours; after that, the learning phase – or critical period – abruptly ends. The imprinted object is normally a living being, but it can be anything that moves. Lorenz imprinted some of his goslings on a bright red ball.

MOTHER FIGURE Staggering to its feet, a newly born wildebeest follows its mother – the first large moving object that it sees when it tumbles into the world.

TWO-WAY EXCHANGE Family attachment works two ways, because parents and offspring have to recognise each other. Here, a female harp seal touches noses with her recently born pup lying on the Arctic ice.

SHARP-EARED PARENTS Gannets nest in crowded colonies that can contain tens of thousands of birds. Even so, every parent instinctively learns to recognise its chick – mainly by imprinting on its call.

Young birds imprint on their parents by sight and sound, but young mammals often imprint on their mother's smell. Shrews are almost blind and cannot see their mother, but they follow her by using their noses. In many grazing mammals, such as wildebeest, calves use hearing as well as smell to identify their mother in a herd.

Wildebeest calves stay with their mothers, but in young gazelles and deer instinct makes a young animal lie low when its mother is not nearby. These young animals are fed by their mothers for less than an hour a day, and between visits they hide. Survival depends on recognising the mother as soon as she arrives and quickly hiding again when she leaves.

FACTS

FARMYARD CHICKS IMPRINT MOST STRONGLY 15 HOURS after they have hatched. After about 30 hours, their imprinting instinct fades away.

A RUFFED GROUSE WAS DISCOVERED IN THE 1960s that had imprinted on a tractor. When the grouse was adult, it tried to court the tractor as a mate.

FEMALE BATS use echolocation to identify their offspring, sometimes from more than 100 000 young crowded together deep in a dark cave.

FACTS

FEEDING

TO FEED THEIR YOUNG, A MALE AND FEMALE GREAT TIT make over 1000 return trips to their nest every day. Their dedication is triggered by powerful instincts – ones that keep them busy from the moment their nestlings hatch. Together, the two birds feed their young for about 18 days. During that time they may clock up over 300 hours of flying time and cover a total distance of nearly 1500 km. For small birds, this is an astounding outlay of energy, but many other birds and mammals are almost as tireless in feeding their families. Their parenting instincts are switched on by their newborn young or nestlings, which have strong feeding instincts of their own.

Newly hatched great tits are blind, so they cannot see their parents when they arrive with food. Instead, they feel the movement when one of their parents lands, and they react instantly, cheeping loudly and stretching upwards with gaping beaks. Compared to the rest of their bodies, their gaping beaks are enormous; they are also funnel-shaped and colourful, making them impossible to miss. The parent bird drops food into whichever one begs the hardest, and then flies off to find the next delivery. Meanwhile, the young birds fall silent and huddle together – an instinct that helps to conceal the whereabouts of the nest.

Compared to young great tits, young herring gulls are much more developed when they hatch. They can see, and they have a covering of fluffy down. Instead of begging at random, herring-gull chicks respond to the shape of the parent's beak, pecking at a red mark just below the tip. This instinct is so powerful that they will peck at a model beak for hours, even though it never produces any food.

A liquid diet

Young mammals are born with a powerful suckling instinct that enables them to feed on their mother's milk. When a mammal starts suckling – often just minutes after being born – the pressure triggers the release of oxytocin, a hormone produced in the mother's brain. Oxytocin is carried around the mother's body in her blood. When it arrives at her mammary glands, it acts like a switch, turning on the flow of milk.

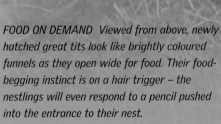

FOOD ON DEMAND Viewed from above, newly hatched great tits look like brightly coloured funnels as they open wide for food. Their food-begging instinct is on a hair trigger – the nestlings will even respond to a pencil pushed into the entrance to their nest.

FROM BIRTH TO WEANING A young manatee suckles milk from its mother in the waterways of Florida. By the time the calf is 18 months old, its mother will have stopped producing milk, forcing it to find its own food.

All female mammals produce milk, but their feeding patterns vary. Young whales can feed at any time because they are at their mother's side. Whale milk is so rich that a blue whale calf can grow by 90 kg a day. But in relative terms, seals grow even faster: drinking milk, a seal pup can double its weight in under a week. In horses, the doubling time is eight weeks, and in humans it is nearly six months. But not all young mammals can feed on demand. Young hares, or leverets, feed for just five minutes a day. For the rest of the time, their instincts keep them perfectly still, hidden away in tall grass.

Accidents and deceit

As young birds and mammals develop, their parents' feeding behaviour changes, preparing the young for the time when they will feed themselves. Some seabirds – including puffins – simply abandon their young after a set time, forcing them to leave the nest and set out to sea. Female mammals gradually stop producing milk, weaning their young onto solid food. But occasionally, instinct gets it wrong. In one famous example, an American cardinal bird was spotted feeding goldfish at the edge of a garden pool. The fish were used to being fed by humans, and the bird's feeding instincts were triggered by their open mouths.

This kind of behaviour is very unusual, but some birds – notably cuckoos – turn other birds' instincts to their own advantage when they breed. The cuckoo lays its eggs in other birds' nests, and the unwitting foster parents raise the young cuckoo as if it was their own. Amazingly, the foster parents do not seem to realise they have been tricked, and they keep supplying the impostor with food. They continue doing this even when the young cuckoo is several times their size, and so big that it no longer fits inside their nest.

DEFENDING THE YOUNG

IN NATURE, EVEN THE MOST PLACID PARENTS CAN REACT WITH FURY IF THEIR YOUNG ARE THREATENED. Heavyweight animals, such as elephants, intervene with devastating strength, but smaller parents also have ways of preventing their young coming to harm. These defensive instincts are extremely powerful, and they are not directed only towards alien species. Female

mammals – from baboons to bears – guard their young from any adult that makes the mistake of venturing too close. When danger strikes, parental ties are paramount in deciding exactly who defends whom.

Most female animals take risks to save their own young, but ignore young belonging to others, even if they could do something to help. The same is true of helping other adults – nature's rule of thumb is that everyone looks after themselves. The major exceptions are social species – those that live in groups where everyone is closely related. An elephant herd is a

social group spanning several generations, which helps to explain why the adults work together to protect each other's young. Groups of smaller animals, such as meerkats and kookaburras, behave in a similar way. Kookaburras live in extended families, consisting of two breeding adults and several helpers – normally, their grown-up young. If anything dangerous enters the family's territory, the young helpers are often the first to attack.

Fighting back

When a young animal is threatened, instinct can make the mother react with remarkable ferocity. It is normal for wild boar to be wary of humans, but they have been known to kill when defending their young. Grazing mammals, such as antelope, sometimes lunge at predators with their horns, while female cats lash out with their claws. Even something as small as a shrew will fight to protect its young, sinking its teeth into animals many times its own size.

Birds have fewer weapons, but they can be just as determined at fighting back. Geese are famously aggressive when they have goslings, while gulls and terns are even more fearless in fending off attacks. These birds dive-bomb their enemies, instinctively swooping down from behind. The effect is like a fighter plane bursting out of the sky: as the bird flies past, it screeches and often rakes the intruder with its beak or feet. Apart from bugs, earwigs and scorpions, very few invertebrates take any interest in their own young, and even fewer defend them from attack. But there is one important and fascinating exception: social insects, which include termites, bees, ants and wasps. These animals live in giant family groups, and they retaliate without fear or hesitation. If their nest is attacked, thousands of insects pour out, ready to defend it to the death.

In the animal world, this kind of suicidal valour is extremely rare. When the worst comes to the worst, most animals instinctively know when to give up the fight, so that they have a chance of breeding again. So why do social insects seem so ready to take this ultimate step? The answer, scientists believe, lies in the unique way these insects breed.

In a honeybee nest, only the queen lays eggs. She has a normal double set of genes, but her male partner has just one. Most of her eggs hatch into female workers, which do not breed, while a handful produce new queens. A small number produce new males, or drones, whose only job is to breed. Unlike normal sisters, the workers and new queens share three-quarters of their genes, and the new queens pass on these genes when they breed. This means that the workers pass on more genes by helping the queens and defending the nest than they would if

MOTHER ON GUARD A furious warthog confronts a martial eagle intent on attacking its injured piglet lying in the grass.

they could breed themselves. Worker honeybees, of course, know nothing about genetics, but this remarkable breeding system has proved to be an incredible success. When social insects defend their nests, they are simply obeying their instincts – but those instincts have made them into some of the most widespread species on Earth.

Moving out

Many animal parents do not have the advantage of superior numbers or strength, and go out of their way to avoid fighting to protect their young. When danger threatens, they use stealth or deception instead. The commonest instinct in these situations – shared by parents of all kinds – is to move the young somewhere else. Cats of all sizes, from tabbies to tigers, do this if their lair is disturbed. The mother picks up the kitten or cub by the scruff of its neck, which triggers a reflex that makes it go limp. She carries the entire litter, one at a time, to a new place, using a gentle version of the grip that she uses when carrying prey.

Dogs and foxes also carry their young this way, but moving a family is more difficult for birds. Only a few species – including water rails and gallinules – can carry their young in their beaks, and only a handful can safely lift them with their feet. But waterbirds are more fortunate: many can move their entire family by carrying them on their backs. The young birds usually just sit tight, but baby grebes grip their parent's feathers with their beaks so they stay in place even if the parent dives.

Mouthbrooding cichlids of East Africa, which demonstrate some of the most intensive parenting among fish, have a snappier technique for moving a whole family at

> **The purple sandpiper carries out a variation on the distraction display, called a 'rodent run'. Dragging both its wings and raising its feathers like fur, it scampers off like a real rodent, squealing as it goes.**

once. The father opens his mouth and the young swim inside. He then shuts his mouth and swims away.

Follow me

Ground-nesting birds face special problems looking after their eggs and chicks. Their nests are easy for predators – both mammals and other birds – to get at, and easy for large animals to step on by mistake. Without emergency action, eggs and young alike can be flattened in an instant. If something dangerous comes nearby, these birds often confront their enemy, calling loudly and flapping their wings. If confrontation is unsuccessful, the parent tries a distraction display.

The most impressive distraction displays are staged by waders, such as curlews, plovers and lapwings, which are preyed on by crows, foxes, stoats and rats. The parent bird lands on the ground between the nest and the intruder and behaves as if it is injured, spreading its tail and trailing one of its wings. It then scurries over the ground, all the while heading away from the nest. Small waders, such as the purple sandpiper, carry out a variation on this display, called a 'rodent run'. Dragging both its wings and raising its feathers like fur, a sandpiper scampers off like a real rodent, squealing as it goes. With both displays, the effect is the same: they attract the intruder's attention and – with luck – lure it away from the eggs or young.

Distraction displays are instinctive, but they can be so convincing that it is hard not to believe that the bird knows what it is doing. If the intruder lags behind, the 'injured' bird will even stop to let it catch up. The moment the trespasser is a safe distance from the nest, the bird miraculously recovers and flies back to its young.

EMERGENCY ESCAPE A tiger cub instinctively stays silent while its mother carries it to safety. Instinct also stops it wandering off while the tigress collects its brothers and sisters.

BLOCKING THE WAY Spreading their wings wide, two bustards try to prevent a young crocodile from raiding their nest. This behaviour makes them look bigger and more threatening than they really are.

GROWING UP

A BABY CHIMPANZEE CLINGS TO ITS MOTHER FOR ITS FIRST SIX MONTHS, and suckles her milk for at least four years. This long childhood – one of the longest after humans' – explains why chimpanzees learn so much from each other. In the animal world, few parents stay with their young for anything like this time. Wildebeest are adult by the time they are three years old, and even blue whales finish suckling before they are a year old, although they can live for over 100 years. But for primates, including chimps and humans, childhood is a time to acquire special skills – a process that takes time.

A young wildebeest does not have to learn much about feeding because there is just one item on its menu – and grass is easy to find. But for hunters and omnivorous

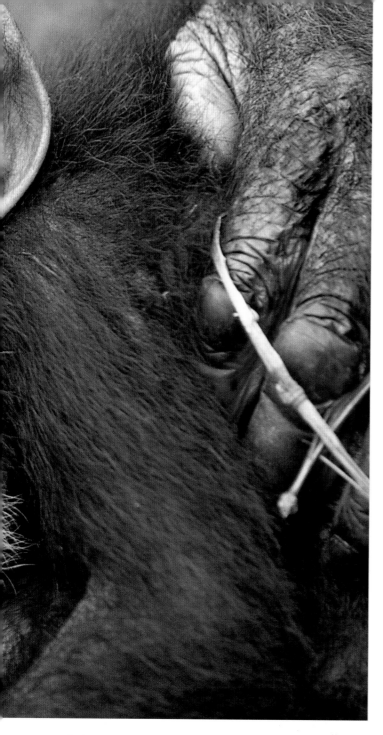

BABE IN ARMS Few instincts are as strong as those that bind female mammals and their young. During its long childhood, this young chimp will instinctively turn to its mother for food and protection.

they are attacked or when they hunt. Chimp troops hunt using a mixture of pursuit and ambush, tactics that have to be learned carefully by individual members if they are to work.

Animals at play

There is something irresistibly appealing about watching young animals playing. Kittens chase anything small that moves, while fox cubs chase their tails. Young elephants throw sticks, attack non-existent enemies and take turns to clamber over each other while they roll on the ground. To us it looks like simple high spirits, but for many mammals it is an important part of growing up. Play allows young animals to practise important skills, and teaches them how to interact with their own kind.

Much more puzzling, as far as scientists are concerned, is play that involves adults. Adult dolphins are extraordinarily playful, in the wild and in captivity. Adult otters are just as lively: their particular favourite is making mud slides on river banks. Even adult birds can be playful. Eider ducks have been seen 'white water rafting', while crows and their relatives are notorious for playing with sticks and wires. Why do adult animals do this? The official answer is that they are simply following playful instincts. The unofficial answer is just for fun.

LOOK AND LEARN Watching attentively, a chimp in West Africa sees how another uses a stone as a tool. For chimps, seeing something done is only a short step away from trying it for themselves.

animals, finding food and dealing with it often needs more than instinct. Peregrine falcons – the world's fastest fliers – hatch with an instinct to pursue other birds, but to become effective hunters they have to be trained by their parents. While young peregrines are still at the nest, the adults will sometimes catch a bird and coax the nestlings by dropping the carcass through the air. With a top airspeed of 230 km/h, the young have to master the art of diving onto their prey without risking a crash.

Chimps are omnivores, so have even more to learn. By watching their parents, they find out how to use tools, such as sticks for collecting termites from termite mounds and stones for smashing open nuts. In some parts of central Africa, chimps smash nuts on stone 'anvils' that have been worn down over many generations – evidence of local traditions that are decades or even centuries old. Finally, young chimps have to learn how to work as part of a troop – a skill that is particularly important if

FINDING FOOD

5

HUNGER RULES THE ANIMAL WORLD. Some animals never eat after becoming adult, but for most, life is driven by the urge to find food. Instinct plays a large part in telling an animal where to look for food as well as how to gather or catch it. It also tells animals what not to eat, and even guides them to food that will keep them healthy. For some creatures, instinct is all they need for finding food, but others – including predators like lions, which hunt in groups – display behaviour that involves learning from others to some degree. When a pride of lions stalk prey, they are taking part in a deadly battle of competing instincts, because the animals they hunt have instincts, too. Animals have evolved a whole range of defences against predators, including camouflage and mimicry, in their never-ending fight for survival.

THE HUNT FOR FOOD

BURSTING UPWARDS THROUGH THE SEA'S SURFACE, A GREAT WHITE SHARK DWARFS A YOUNG FUR SEAL DESTINED TO BECOME ITS NEXT MEAL. The great white is the ultimate pursuit predator, tracking down its prey by sensing vibrations and by using its astounding sense of smell. The great white's sense of smell is unbelievably acute, and its hunting instincts are often activated while it is still several kilometres from its prey. Great whites also sense where the scent is coming from. As soon as the shark picks up the scent, instinct makes it turn and head towards the source. Like most fish, sharks are also equipped with a fluid-filled canal, called a lateral line, which runs along their sides. This contains nerves that detect low-frequency vibrations – the kind given off by inexperienced or injured animals, such as hooked fish or playful seals. Sharks can navigate using their vibration sense alone, which explains how they are able to attack in blood-stained water, or after dark.

By the time a shark makes eye contact with its prey, escape is often impossible and the animal's fate is sealed. In contrast, for land predators such as cats and dogs, it is the sight of a moving creature, rather than its scent or sound, that triggers the instinct to chase and attack. Hunters such as lions and cheetahs hunt gazelle, antelope and other grazers, which are alert and have quick escape responses. Cover on the African plains is sparse, and predators need to pick an individual from a distance and close in undetected to have any chance of success. The cheetah's excellent eyesight enables it to choose a victim from up to 5 km away. It then stalks its prey until it is close enough to break cover in a short burst of speed. However, it takes more than speed and keen eyesight to catch an agile gazelle. From an early age, the cubs of predator species watch their mothers hunting, and imitate the way she stalks prey, makes outflanking manoeuvres and goes for the kill. And in species that hunt in groups or packs, the young and inexperienced members take their lead from the experienced, and so acquire the tactics needed for the group to succeed.

Giant killer

The record for the largest predator that actively pursues individual prey is held by the sperm whale, a hunter that can weigh over 50 tonnes. Remarkably, the sperm whale shows no aggressive instincts towards man. At the surface, these giant predators lounge almost motionless and seem oblivious to divers inspecting their heads and their jaws. Despite centuries of whaling, there has been only one authenticated case of a sperm whale causing serious loss of human life – and even then, it did not kill directly. The attack, on the whaler *Essex* in 1820, sank the ship and left the crew adrift in the Pacific Ocean. After three months at sea, with little food or water, only a handful of them survived.

THE FINAL ACT Tossed about like a plaything, a young fur seal is little more than a snack for a fully grown great white shark. The shark throws its prey around to stun it, then swallows it whole.

ANTS

THE LARGEST HUNTING PACKS IN THE ANIMAL WORLD ARE COLUMNS OF ARMY ANTS IN TROPICAL RAIN FORESTS. A SINGLE SWARM CAN CONTAIN UP TO 2 MILLION ANTS, MARCHING IN A COLUMN UP TO 100 M LONG. The ants fan out as they spread across the ground, scuttling over fallen leaves and climbing to the tops of the highest trees. As the swarm surges forwards, the ants kill and eat anything too slow to escape. Their victims include other insects, spiders and worms, and occasionally frogs, lizards and poisonous snakes. They are slow to harm humans, but they sometimes attack tethered farm animals, and there are even reports of swarms invading remote towns. Army ants are almost blind, and they find their prey by touch. If one ant finds food, it instinctively releases a chemical signal or pheromone, which brings other ants rushing to the spot. Using this communication system, a single ant can 'recruit' hundreds of others from several metres away.

The swarm's activity is divided into two phases, which alternate at intervals of between two and three weeks. During the nomadic stage, the ants set off at dawn and pitch a temporary camp at night. This camp – known as a bivouac – is often under a fallen tree and consists of a ball of ants linked together by their feet. The other phase is the breeding stage, during which the bivouac stays in one place, allowing the queen enough time to lay large numbers of eggs. When the nomadic stage resumes, the queen and her young travel at the rear, surrounded by a retinue of guards. The ants are not alone on the move. Antbirds are instinctively drawn to a swarm and flutter near the front of the column, snapping up insects driven out of hiding by the ants.

CLASS: Insecta
ORDER: Hymenoptera
SPECIES: *Eciton* (American army ants), *Dorylus* (African army ants or driver ants)
HABITAT: Tropical forest
DISTRIBUTION: Central and South America, Central Africa
KEY FEATURES: Slender-bodied ants with a nomadic hunting lifestyle; breed in temporary bivouacs rather than permanent nests

VITAL STATISTICS

BON APPETIT A gaboon viper devours a rodent whole. The prey does not struggle because it is already dead, killed by a venomous bite.

CONTRASTING STRATEGIES

TRACKING DOWN PREY INDIVIDUALLY CAN BE A COSTLY WAY OF LIFE. A predator may spend hours closing in on food, only to lose its quarry at the last moment when it launches the attack. For a cheetah or a polar bear, failure is a serious business, particularly in the breeding season when the female has a young family to feed.

The world's largest predators get around this problem by feeding in bulk. A blue whale feeds on krill – small crustaceans that thrive in icy seas. Krill are only about 6 cm long, but they form vast swarms that can weigh over a million tonnes. This mass of small animals makes feeding easy: the whale simply cruises through a swarm with its mouth open and its throat inflated like a balloon. Having taken a mouthful, it then closes its jaws and tightens its throat to squeeze out the water, leaving the krill behind. Once the filtering is complete, the whale swallows its prey – up to a quarter of a tonne at a time.

This way of living, called filter-feeding, is the most energy-efficient that evolution has devised. Blue whales do not need instinctive skills for concealment or cunning. They just plough their way through their food, like a farmer harvesting a crop.

Sit-and-wait hunters

Filter-feeding is viable in the ocean, but it does not work on land. Here, many predators use a different strategy: they keep still and wait for their prey to come to them. Sit-and-wait predators can be incredibly patient, but the moment something edible comes within reach, instinct triggers a lightning response. The gaboon viper from West Africa is one of the world's most dangerous sit-and-wait snakes, with a deadly habit of lying on forest paths. It is rarely more than 1.5 m long, but its thickset body can be as fat as a human leg. Decorated with an intricate geometric pattern, it looks conspicuous in the open, but is almost invisible curled up among fallen leaves. The viper's sluggish behaviour belies its extraordinarily rapid reactions: if it senses vibrations from approaching feet, it can strike in less than a second, delivering venom through a pair of fangs measuring up to 5 cm long. Like most vipers, it instinctively releases its grip after this initial strike, reducing its chances of being injured while the venom does its deadly work.

The sit-and-wait strategy is used by many small land animals, from spiders to praying mantises. But for rapid reactions, none of these can beat predators that lurk in shallow seas. Frogfish attract their prey by waving a fleshy lure, which dangles enticingly in front of their mouths. If another fish comes within range, the frogfish's mouth suddenly opens like a trapdoor, sucking its victim inside. This movement can take place in just 0.006 seconds – so fast it cannot be seen with the naked eye.

Frogfish hold the record for the quickest movement among vertebrates (animals with backbones), but stomatopods or mantis shrimps are faster still. Their barbed front legs can impale a fish in just 0.004 seconds – one of the fastest animal movements known. Their instinctive response is so strong that they will attack almost anything that comes within range – including divers careless enough to poke their fingers into a stomatopod's lair.

FOOD RECOGNITION

ON A RIVER BANK IN THE SOUTH AMERICAN RAIN FOREST, A FRINGE-LIPPED BAT SWOOPS DOWN TO CATCH A CROAKING FROG. The frog looks like an easy catch, but at the very last moment the bat suddenly swerves and flies away. Why? The answer lies in the way animals recognise their food. Fringe-lipped bats often hunt ground-dwelling animals, which they locate by sound. When a bat hears a frog croaking, it instinctively locks on to the sound and flies down to attack. But in this case, the frog has a special defence: its skin is

moment when the frog appears literally to be staring death in the face, the bat catches this scent and realises its mistake.

For animals that hunt, recognising appropriate and safe food is a complex business – and there are serious penalties for getting things wrong. Predators have to know which species are good to eat and which ones are dangerous and need to be avoided. Fringe-lipped bats often feed on frogs, but are able to distinguish between the kinds that are edible and the ones that are best left alone.

Picky eaters

Food recognition instincts can be rough and ready, or remarkably precise. Bullfrogs will eat almost anything that moves, as long as they can fit it in their mouths. Foxes and raccoons will try all

CLOSE CALL In the animal world, few near-death experiences come as close as this. Protected by its chemical defences, a tropical frog sits tight as a bat swoops down, attracted by its croaking. The bat realises its error just in time, and stops short of biting the poisonous creature.

kinds of natural food and human leftovers, as will gulls and polar bears. Sharks are even less discriminating. They eat anything that smells even faintly edible, from bags that contain fish waste to empty drums of cooking oil. Small sharks, such as the cookiecutter, have been known to bite chunks from the plastic sleeves of cables on the seafloor.

At the other extreme, some animals start life with an amazing ability to recognise specific kinds of food. For example, the chicks of tropical herons instinctively know the difference between poisonous sea snakes and edible eels. Many other birds instinctively recognise stinging insects. So do spiders that catch them in their webs. If a spider nets a wasp, it gets within touching distance, but then retreats as fast as it can. If a wasp does not free itself, the spider will sometimes wrap it in silk, before cutting it out of the web so that it drops harmlessly to the ground.

Parasites are even better at telling one kind of animal from another. Many parasitic insects lay their eggs on other insects' grubs. These parasites are amazingly selective. Using their sense of smell, many of them instinctively search out just one kind of host – behaviour that makes them extremely useful for controlling insect pests. Bird lice are just as choosy: many species live on just one species of bird. Ornithologists can sometimes use these parasites to unravel puzzles in bird evolution, because birds and their lice have evolved together over thousands or even millions of years.

Acquired tastes

This inherited choosiness is quite different from food recognition that is learned. Mammals and ground-nesting birds often learn about food by watching their parents eat. Songbirds do not have such a long training period, because they stay in their nests while their parents are out foraging. As a result, they have to learn more about food for themselves.

In North America, young blue jays quickly learn that some butterflies are good to eat, but that there is a catch with one common butterfly – the monarch, which contains poisons called glycosides. If a jay catches and eats a monarch, it soon discovers its mistake and coughs it up. From that moment onwards, the jay associates this unpleasant experience with monarchs and avoids all butterflies that have the monarch's colour scheme, with bright orange and black wings. The monarch's bright colours are no accident: they have evolved to show blue jays and other predators that they eat the butterfly at their peril.

Monarch butterflies are not the only animals that warn off their enemies in this way. Many poisonous animals, from bumblebees to coral snakes, display warning colours: black and yellow for bumblebees; red, black and yellow or white for coral snakes. The markings make them easy to recognise and help to keep predators at bay.

The chicks of tropical herons instinctively know the difference between poisonous sea snakes and edible eels. Many other birds instinctively recognise stinging insects. So do spiders that catch them in their webs.

ESCAPE
ARTISTS

WHEN DANGER STRIKES, ANIMALS DO
NOT WASTE TIME DECIDING HOW TO
REACT. Instinct takes control and launches
emergency action straightaway. Whether it involves
dashing for safety or staying absolutely still, this behaviour helps
to save animals from becoming someone else's meal.

For sheer acceleration, few escape artists can beat the
common housefly. Its brain is minute, but it has unusually large
eyes and its body bristles with sensitive hairs. If anything
approaches the fly once it has settled, its eyes instantly
register the changing light levels and its hairs pick up telltale
currents in the air. These sensory signals activate its thoracic
muscles, rapidly powering up its wings. The fly stows away its
mouthparts and pushes upwards with its legs, and in less than
half a second it is in the air. Instinct then guides it towards the
lightest part of the horizon – usually the best direction for
steering clear of harm.

Doing a runner

The laws of physics mean that small animals like the housefly are
amazingly good at accelerating from a standing start. On the other
hand, their top speed is often quite slow. A housefly rarely flies

faster than about 10 km/h, while a cockroach, despite being the
fastest sprinter in the insect world, manages only about 5 km/h.
But for these creatures, manoeuvrability is as important as speed.
Unlike larger animals, they can change direction almost instantly
because their bodies weigh so little. Their instincts exploit this to
the full, giving them a jerky and unpredictable movement that
makes them difficult to catch.

In the arms race between predator and prey, many
vertebrates use similar tactics, even though their size means that
they are not quite so nimble. Hares run off in one direction, then
double back, while snipe follow a zig-zag path through the sky.
Antelope twist and swerve when pursued by cheetahs, turning
sharp corners at over 60 km/h. If the antelope sets off with a
good head start, this is is often enough to throw off a cheetah.

The plumed baselisk lizard of the American tropics has a
startling and impressive escape technique – it runs on water.
When threatened by a predator, it drops out of trees into rivers,
then races across the surface on its powerful back legs. Adult
basilisks cannot keep this up for more than a few strides, but
young ones are light enough to 'walk on water' for over 20 m,
hence the species' alternative name of the Jesus Christ lizard.

Diving for cover

In an emergency, many animals head to a safe refuge, where
predators cannot follow them. Small mammals often disappear
into burrows, while fish vanish into crevices in coral reefs. Ducks
and geese head out into open water, leaving dry-land predators

*SAFETY ON TWO LEGS Running on its hindlegs,
a basilisk lizard can cross the water's surface at
12 km/h. It has webbed toes on its back feet,
which work like a pair of paddles. When it sinks,
it swims away powered by its tail.*

behind. Some waterbirds – particularly gulls – use water as a refuge when they roost at night. They stream inland to gather on lakes and lagoons, and then fly back out to the coast at dawn.

Freeze!

Freezing is an instinctive reaction that many animals share. It can put a predator off an animal's track – or at least buy vital time. Frogs and toads, for example, cannot recognise motionless prey. Nor can predatory insects that hunt by sight, such as the praying mantis. A fly is safe sitting next to a mantis: if it moves, it risks being recognised and eaten. Similarly, carnivorous mammals such as cats often lose interest when their prey stays still.

This difference is related to brain size and to the way predators hunt. Cats have well-developed brains and superb eyesight, but they feed exclusively on freshly killed prey so their instincts make them focus on things that move. A praying mantis also has good vision but a small brain. It is good at spotting movement, but its brain does not have enough processing power to perceive motionless shapes as prey.

Birds are a far greater danger to insects because they have enough brain power to spot prey even when it is still. Many insects use camouflage as a defence, but birds are not easily fooled, so insects have evolved some extraordinary disguises. Some mimic leaves, twigs or bark. Others look like insects that taste bad or sting – the hornet clearwing moth is so convincing, it fools most people as well.

Animals under siege

In ancient times, Roman legionnaires protected themselves by forming a 'tortoise', made of interlocking shields. In the animal kingdom, a wide variety of animals use this kind of defence, quite

INWARD STRENGTH When a pill millipede rolls up, its head and legs are completely hidden. The biggest pill millipedes, from South Africa and Australia, can be the size of a golf ball.

apart from tortoises. These animals share two key features: some form of body armour, such as hard plates or spines, and an instinct to hold their ground when attacked, instead of trying to make an escape. For animals such as the three-banded armadillo and the pill millipede, this instinct puts a block on any chance of running away. Although very different in size, both are covered in armour, and if threatened they roll up with their legs and head tucked away. They stay rolled up until all seems quiet, at which point they cautiously relax their guard. As a defence, it has one big advantage: it can be deployed anywhere and at any time. But it is not entirely foolproof. Rolled-up armadillos are easy prey for jaguars, and birds sometimes eat rolled-up pill millipedes, while badgers are not put off by the spines on a curled-up hedgehog. When the predators are humans, the outcome can be much worse. Sailors hunting fresh meat used to prize giant tortoises from remote islands such as the Galápagos and Seychelles. It was all too easy to catch these armoured reptiles, because their instincts stopped them in their tracks the moment they were approached.

SCAVENGERS

BY EATING THE REMAINS OF DEAD AND ROTTING ANIMALS, scavengers help the decomposition process and are vital to the health of an ecosystem. Unlike hunters, they do not need complex instincts for capturing food, but they need to keep ahead of the competition in order to find food before too many others join in. This scramble for first place is particularly important for vultures, because large carcasses tend to be few and far between.

Vultures' eyesight is legendary, but unusually for birds some also have a good sense of smell. The North American turkey vulture has the keenest nose. It is instinctively attracted by the foul-smelling chemicals given off by rotting flesh. One of these 'carcass chemicals', a substance called ethyl mercaptan, is added to natural gas to make leaks easier to find. In the USA, turkey vultures have been seen circling over gas pipelines, instinctively drawn by the smell of ethyl mercaptan escaping into the air.

Vultures can spot food from over 2 km up in the air, but they spend as much time watching each other as watching the ground. When one vulture drops towards a carcass, it triggers others to follow it and eventually these airborne scavengers can

Vultures can spot food from 2 km up in the air, but they spend as much time watching each other as watching the ground.

FIRST COME, FIRST SERVED
White-backed vultures jostle for
their share of a carcass in southern
Africa. With a continuous stream
of birds arriving, there is no time
to be lost. Instinct spurs them
to feed as quickly as they can.

BURYING THE DEAD
Attracted by the smell of dead
flesh, burying beetles examine
the body of a small rodent.
Once they have assessed its
size, they will start digging
it a grave.

DEATH AND REBIRTH **(1)** A pair of burying beetles excavate under a corpse. **(2)** As the corpse sinks, the beetles shape it into a ball. **(3)** The female lays her eggs around the body. When the grubs hatch, the parents help them to feed. **(4)** The grubs change into adults and clamber to the surface.

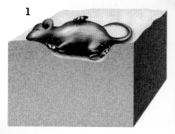

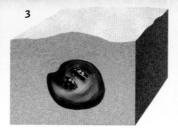

gather from up to 25 km away. In Africa, four kinds of vulture may end up jostling for a meal. When this happens, each kind concentrates on a different part of the carcass. The black vulture tears open the skin; the long-necked griffon vulture reaches deep inside, while the much smaller Egyptian vulture stays further back, feeding on scraps. Finally, the massively built bearded vulture or lammergeier finishes the remains of the feast. It can rip apart sun-dried skin and meat, and by a remarkable instinct picks up bones and drops them onto rocks, smashing them open to reveal the marrow inside.

Beetle teamwork

When vultures feed, there is no holding back: every bird is out for itself. Instinct works very differently with burying beetles, because these nocturnal scavengers often operate as a male and female team. They feed on the corpses of small mammals and birds and bury the remains to act as nurseries for their young.

Burying beetles find corpses by smell. When the beetle couple tracks down a body, they work fast to bury it before any other beetles home in. The first step is to test the soil. If it is too hard, the beetles will often drag the corpse several metres to looser ground. Next, they start digging beneath the body, so that it gradually drops out of sight. As the burial proceeds, the beetles shape the corpse into a ball and remove its feathers or fur. They also cover it with slimy secretions that help to slow down decay. Once the remains are completely buried, the female lays her eggs either on the corpse or in the soil close by. In many species, the two beetles then guard the nursery, feeding the young on

chewed-up remains until they are ready to feed for themselves. Throughout the entire operation, instinct works like an unseen funeral director, ensuring that the burial goes to plan.

Dung beetles

For some scavengers, the search for food focuses on animal droppings rather than dead remains. The yellow dung fly is a common resident on grazing pasture, where it searches out fresh manure. For these flies, piles of fresh manure also act as courtship grounds – an unusual place to look for a mate. Dung beetles, or scarabs, take longer to arrive than flies, and when they do, their instinct is quite different. Instead of feeding on the spot, they mould the dung into little balls and roll them away.

There are many species of dung beetle, and they typically work in male and female pairs. Using their flattened front legs, they pat some dung into a ball. Once it is ready, they move it by heaving with their back legs, while bracing their front legs against the ground. Sometimes both beetles push, but more often one does the rolling, while the other rides on top, dropping down to the ground from time to time to help with the steering. After several metres, they bury the ball, together with a batch of eggs.

This dung-rolling instinct is very important for grassland habitats, because it helps to scatter animal droppings, which break down and fertilise the soil. In Australia, the native beetles avoid cattle droppings, which caused problems for farmers until over 40 species of dung beetle were imported. Nearly half have become established in the wild, and thanks to these industrious insects, Australia's problem with dung is now under control.

PLANT EATERS

WHEN A BUTTERFLY LAYS ITS EGGS, IT CANNOT AFFORD TO MAKE MISTAKES. It must choose exactly the right plant if its caterpillars are to survive. Scientists once thought that butterflies do this by remembering the type of foodplant they grew up on when they were caterpillars. But experiments have shown that instinct – rather than learning – gives butterflies the guidance they need.

Butterflies recognise plants by their shape, colour and, above all, smell. If a plant looks right, a female butterfly will land on a leaf to run a chemical check. Often, it uses its feet to do this. It taps the leaf with its feet, which have tiny spines that prick the surface, allowing some of the leaf's juices to leak out. Chemical detectors that are also on its feet can 'smell' the plant. If the plant contains the right mix of chemicals, the butterfly gets ready to lay. If not, it moves on.

Across the world, there are more than 160 000 types of butterfly and moth, and almost all of their caterpillars feed on plants. Plant-eating insects also include over 75 000 kinds of sap-sucking bugs and a host of other leaf-eaters, from stick insects to grasshoppers and katydids. Together these animals consume billions of tonnes of plant food every year.

Chemical warfare

Not all are choosy about the food that they eat. Woodland moths, for example, often lay their eggs and feed on a wide range of shrubs and trees. But for the great majority of insects, being picky has a big advantage: they become specialists, able to crack the defences of their foodplants. Most plants protect themselves with indigestible chemicals or poisons to keep animals at bay. By concentrating on a single type of plant, animals evolve ways to overcome these defences – and have all the food source to themselves. Some go further: they appropriate the plant's defences. Cabbage white butterflies home in on the scent of mustard oil – a chemical deterrent that gives cabbage leaves their peppery tang. Instead of deterring cabbage whites, the oil attracts them and activates the female's instinct to lay eggs. This instinct is so strong that cabbage whites even lay on pieces of green paper that have been impregnated with the oil.

Insects are not the only plant-eaters that specialise in this way. Giant pandas are just as fussy, and so are Australia's koalas. There are over 600 species of eucalyptus tree in Australia, all of them protected by pungent oils that make their leaves difficult to digest. Koalas can eat them, but they feed on just 30 kinds, turning their noses up at the rest. Their leafy diet is low in energy, which explains why these appealing marsupials spend up to four-fifths

*ATTACK AND DEFENCE While nibbling away
at the edges of a leaf, these tropical caterpillars
react to danger by raising their tails – a trick
that makes them look dangerous.*

**Plant-eating
insects include
the caterpillars of more
than 160 000 types of
butterfly and moth,
over 75 000 kinds of
sap-sucking bugs and a
host of other leaf-eaters.**

HEADS DOWN Grazers – like these zebras and wildebeest – will spend up to half their lives eating.

The herding instinct

Grass is easy to find, so grazing animals do not have to look far for food. It nourishes the biggest concentration of land mammals on the planet, including more than 1.5 million wildebeest in East Africa's Serengeti, which migrate throughout the seasons to keep in step with rain. Even larger herds of grazing mammals existed in the past. Up to 90 million bison once roamed North America's great plains, while in the late 19th century a single herd of springbok seen in South Africa was an incredible 150 km long.

Most grazing mammals share a strong herding instinct, because in a habitat without cover, safety lies in sticking together. A diet of grass affects their behaviour in other ways. Ruminants such as antelope and cattle digest their food with the help of on-board microbes and a complicated digestive system that contains four separate stomach compartments. To make this work, they 'chew the cud', regurgitating their food and chewing it a second time. According to folklore, cows lie down when it is going to rain. What actually happens is that cows, and all other ruminants, feed until their stomachs are full. At this point, instinct make them switch to rumination – something that they often do lying down, whatever the weather has in store.

Storing food

In the distant past, our ancestors discovered that seeds will keep for much longer than most other kinds of food. Some animals, too, instinctively collect seeds and store them for use in hungry times. The record for a single store is held by the common hamster – a close relative of the species kept as pets. One of these rodents was found to have amassed 90 kg of seeds in its burrow, a gigantic stockpile roughly equivalent to 150 times its own weight. The seed-storing instinct runs deep in the hamster family, because they come from places such as Siberia and Mongolia where winters can be severe, or desert regions where food is sparse. Pet hamsters sometimes bury their food in their bedding, even if food supplies are topped up every day.

Apart from rodents, the other leading seed-storers are birds. Acorn woodpeckers work in family groups to store surplus acorns in holes pecked in a dead tree. There may be 50 000 acorns in the tree, so tightly jammed in that it is very difficult for other animals to raid the store. Jays and nutcrackers are also great seed-collectors, but instead of using trees they bury their collection a few seeds at a time. They memorise the location of each cache, finding their stores by remembering the position of nearby landmarks, such as stones. It is an incredible feat, particularly for Clarke's nutcrackers. They store up to 5000 separate caches and can find them again even when the ground is covered by snow.

GIANT
PANDA

CLASS: Mammalia

ORDER: Carnivora

SPECIES: *Ailuropoda melanoleuca*

HABITAT: Bamboo forest

DISTRIBUTION: Central and
western China

KEY FEATURES: Aberrant carnivore
that has evolved a vegetarian diet

ONE OF THE PICKIEST EATERS
**IN THE WHOLE OF THE ANIMAL KINGDOM, THE GIANT
PANDA IS, TECHNICALLY, A CARNIVORE,** but it has evolved to eat
little or no meat. Instead, it survives – just – on a diet of bamboo. This
woody plant is high in fibre, which the panda cannot digest, so it has to
eat a lot – a fully grown giant panda can chew its way through 35 kg of
shoots and leaves in a single day. Most bears have flat paws, which
makes them good at digging but clumsy at picking things up. The panda,
however, has evolved a wrist bone that works like a thumb, helping it to
grip bamboo stems while it feeds. Its teeth are broader than those of
other bears to help with all the chewing, but it still has long canines, or eye-teeth,
showing that its distant ancestors ate meat.

Like most vegetarian creatures, giant pandas spend a lot of time feeding –
sometimes up to 14 hours a day. They live in China's mountain bamboo forests, at altitudes
of up to 3000 m. This habitat has shrunk rapidly during the past 50 years, hence the
panda's adoption as the symbol of threatened wildlife. Despite careful protection, only about
1000 giant pandas still live in the wild. About 150 live in captivity, but even they are under
threat because captive pandas are notoriously reluctant to breed. Scientists have more
recently resorted to trying to clone them, but in the long term this charismatic animal's
survival depends on having enough suitable space in the wild.

NATURAL MEDICINES

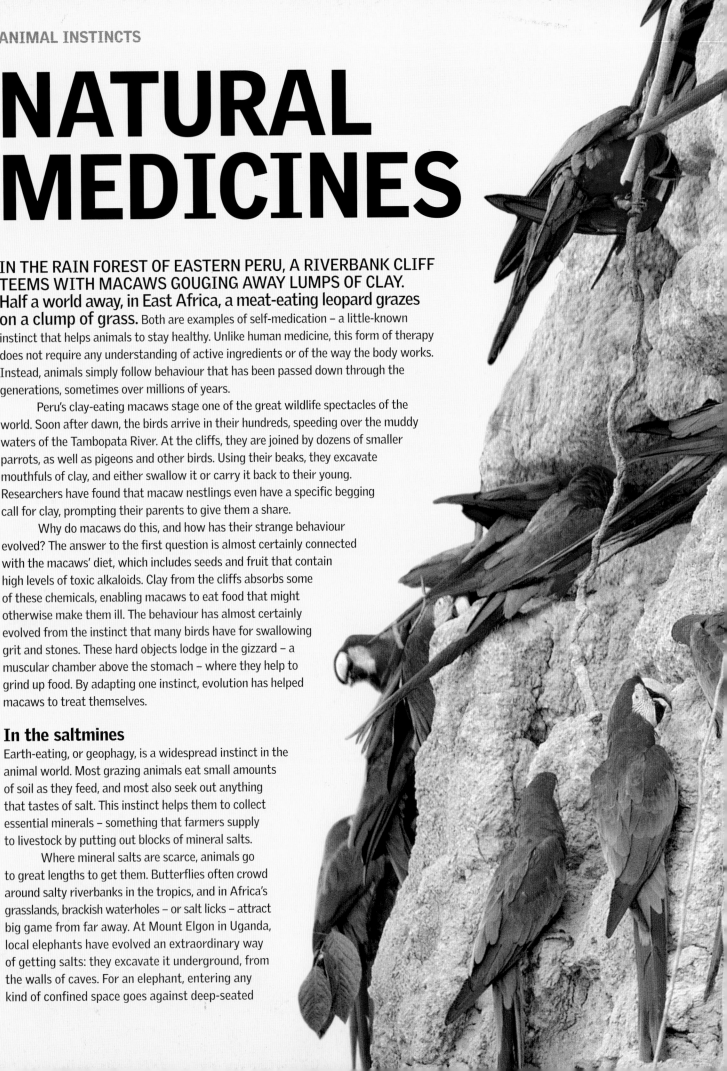

IN THE RAIN FOREST OF EASTERN PERU, A RIVERBANK CLIFF TEEMS WITH MACAWS GOUGING AWAY LUMPS OF CLAY. Half a world away, in East Africa, a meat-eating leopard grazes on a clump of grass. Both are examples of self-medication – a little-known instinct that helps animals to stay healthy. Unlike human medicine, this form of therapy does not require any understanding of active ingredients or of the way the body works. Instead, animals simply follow behaviour that has been passed down through the generations, sometimes over millions of years.

Peru's clay-eating macaws stage one of the great wildlife spectacles of the world. Soon after dawn, the birds arrive in their hundreds, speeding over the muddy waters of the Tambopata River. At the cliffs, they are joined by dozens of smaller parrots, as well as pigeons and other birds. Using their beaks, they excavate mouthfuls of clay, and either swallow it or carry it back to their young. Researchers have found that macaw nestlings even have a specific begging call for clay, prompting their parents to give them a share.

Why do macaws do this, and how has their strange behaviour evolved? The answer to the first question is almost certainly connected with the macaws' diet, which includes seeds and fruit that contain high levels of toxic alkaloids. Clay from the cliffs absorbs some of these chemicals, enabling macaws to eat food that might otherwise make them ill. The behaviour has almost certainly evolved from the instinct that many birds have for swallowing grit and stones. These hard objects lodge in the gizzard – a muscular chamber above the stomach – where they help to grind up food. By adapting one instinct, evolution has helped macaws to treat themselves.

In the saltmines

Earth-eating, or geophagy, is a widespread instinct in the animal world. Most grazing animals eat small amounts of soil as they feed, and most also seek out anything that tastes of salt. This instinct helps them to collect essential minerals – something that farmers supply to livestock by putting out blocks of mineral salts.

Where mineral salts are scarce, animals go to great lengths to get them. Butterflies often crowd around salty riverbanks in the tropics, and in Africa's grasslands, brackish waterholes – or salt licks – attract big game from far away. At Mount Elgon in Uganda, local elephants have evolved an extraordinary way of getting salts: they excavate it underground, from the walls of caves. For an elephant, entering any kind of confined space goes against deep-seated

OPEN-AIR PHARMACY *Clinging to a cliff in the Peruvian Amazon, green macaws help themselves to its medicinal clay to counter toxins in their diet. Birds are not alone in using clay – for centuries, people have used it in traditional remedies, and it remains a common ingredient in some modern medicines.*

MEDICINES FROM THE WILD

In addition to consuming their normal foods, animals eat a wide range of substances that seem to play a part in keeping them healthy. Some of these work as dietary supplements – the equivalent of vitamin or mineral pills. Others seem to be used as emergency treatments when animals fall ill.

SUBSTANCE	SOURCE	EFFECTS	USED BY
Kaolin	Clay	Kaolin absorbs toxic chemicals in an animal's digestive tract, preventing the animal from being poisoned by substances in its food.	Mammals, birds
Silica	Grass	Indigestible crystals of silica help to dislodge intestinal parasites.	Carnivorous mammals
Alkaloids	Plants, especially nightshades	Many alkaloids are potent painkillers and are used in human medicine. Some also help to keep parasites under control.	Mammals, insects
Common salt	Salt licks	An essential part of animal diets. Animals use salt licks in regions where their food is lacking in salt.	Mammals, reptiles
Iodine	Salt licks, seaweed	An essential mineral needed for normal growth. Seaweeds concentrate iodine by collecting it from seawater.	Grazing mammals
Formic acid	Ants	A toxic chemical used by ants in their stings, formic acid may help birds to remove parasites from their plumage.	Birds
Antibiotics	Earth	Produced by microscopic fungi living in soil and on plants, antibiotics kill infectious bacteria.	Mammals, birds

instincts. But the herd instinct is even stronger, and once the lead elephant enters the mouth of the cave, the others follow. When they reach the workface, the elephants lever out the rock with their tusks, before crunching it up with their massive teeth. An elephant needs about a cupful of mineral salts a day, and each one eats enough to keep it going for at least a week. After several hours underground, the herd heads back to the outside world.

Tusk marks and fallen rock shows that Mount Elgon's elephants have been trekking underground like this for many thousands of years. The elephants have an instinctive craving for salt, but they are not born with the knowledge of where to find it. Instead, that is passed on through experience, from the moment each young calf takes its first hesitant steps underground.

Animal herbalists

From time to time, even the most dedicated carnivores can be seen taking mouthfuls of plant food. Cats, from domestic cats to lions, leopards and tigers, are particularly attracted to grass. Because cats cannot digest grass, it often acts as an emetic, making them regurgitate whatever they have recently eaten. If this does not happen, the grass passes almost intact through their bodies, scouring their intestines like a brush. This can help to dislodge intestinal parasites, which often infect carnivores via their food.

There is also evidence that animals instinctively select medicinal plants when they fall ill or as preventive medicines. In South America, monkeys are known to feed on the bark of the cinchona tree, which contains a drug that fights malaria, while several kinds of mammal have been seen wiping themselves with leaves that deter biting insects. In Tanzania, scientists studying chimpanzees watched a sick female as she searched out a small shrub and carefully ate its inner pith. A day later, her symptoms had disappeared and she was moving at the front of her troop. The shrub – known in English as bitter leaf – is used as medicine in tropical Africa to reduce fever and counteract parasites. Like many medicines, its taste is offputting, but chimps seem to know when eating the plant will do them good.

Bathing in ants

Letting ants crawl over your body does not sound like a recipe for good health, but more than 200 species of bird, including jays, starlings and crows, regularly use ants for a strange form of treatment. Some birds use their beaks to pick up stinging ants and wipe them over their feathers. Others spread their wings to encourage ants to climb aboard. While they are doing this, they often quiver their feathers – something that encourages the ants to squirt formic acid from their stings.

'Anting' – as it is called – is fascinating to watch, but not quite so easy to explain. Ornithologists have put forward several theories, including the suggestion that it gives birds an erotic thrill. But most experts believe that anting is a form of self-medication that helps birds to rid themselves of external parasites on their bodies and their wings.

USING TOOLS

TOOL-USERS INCLUDE THE BRIGHTEST AND MOST INGENIOUS MEMBERS OF THE ANIMAL KINGDOM. But there is a huge gulf between animals that instinctively use tools and the gifted few who seem to understand how they work. In 2002, a New Caledonian crow called Betty astounded scientists by showing exactly what this difference means.

Betty had been raised in captivity and was no stranger to intelligence tests. To see quite how inventive she was, researchers presented Betty and her mate with a bucket of food at the bottom of a piece of transparent pipe. The bucket had a handle, but the pipe was too narrow for the crows to reach inside. The research team also gave them two pieces of wire – a straight one and one ending in a hook. The male bird flew off with the hook without getting at the bucket. But Betty took the straight wire, made a hook of her own and pulled the bucket out of the tube. Crows are known for their intelligence, but Betty's achievement catapulted her into a category formerly reserved for the brainiest primates, including chimps and ourselves.

Tool use is more common among captive animals than those living in the wild. But in the bird world, it happens even in the wild. Wild parrots sometimes use sticks to scratch themselves, and woodpecker finches from the Galápagos islands use cactus spines to tweak insect grubs out of their holes.

The best-known tool-using bird is the Egyptian vulture from Europe, Africa and Asia, which uses stones to smash open ostrich shells – after several direct hits, the egg cracks open and the vulture gets its meal. Ornithologists have investigated this egg-cracking behaviour closely to see exactly what it involves. The vulture certainly uses stones as tools, though it does not try to shape them in any way. But does it understand what it is doing, as Betty seems to have done when she made her hook? The answer appears to be no. Often, a vulture throws the stone beside the egg, or in the opposite direction, suggesting that it is not quite so bright after all – or it may simply need more practice.

Betty's behaviour involved insight, but the vulture's egg-cracking behaviour seems to be based on the 'smash and grab'

GENTLY DOES IT
Holding a stick in its beak, a New Caledonian crow dislodges an insect grub from a fallen tree. The stick has to be of exactly the right size.

instinct that many birds share. For example, thrushes often pick up snails and smash them on large stones, while gulls smash crabs on rocks. Egyptian vultures do the same with small eggs, by picking them up in their beaks and giving them a sharp downward flick. Ostrich eggs are far too big for them to deal with in this way, so they evolved the technique of throwing stones at the egg, rather than throwing the egg at stones – a lucky break in a literal way. Once one vulture made the discovery, perhaps accidentally, the behaviour seems to have spread through example and imitation.

The floating kitchen

Off the west coast of North America, sea otters also use stones when they feed, but they do so in a much more versatile way in order to deal with different kinds of prey. Sea otters spend their whole lives offshore, where they feed on shellfish and crustaceans. Abalones are one of their favourite foods, but these saucer-sized molluscs can be a challenge to collect, because they clamp themselves to rocks on the seabed with a powerful sucker up to 10 cm across. To dislodge an abalone, a sea otter collects a stone from the seabed and pounds it against the shell. The otter has to surface for air every minute or so, but returns to its pounding and eventually the abalone loosens its hold and the otter gets its meal.

To break open shellfish such as abalone and clams, a sea otter uses stones in a way that has no direct parallels elsewhere in the animal world. It dives down and picks up a large flat stone, which it tucks under its armpit while it collects food in its paws. Back at the surface, it turns on its back and places the stone on its chest. Using this anvil, it smashes open its food and throws the broken shells overboard. Sea otters do seem to have insight into what they are doing, even though they do not shape their tools. They are the only mammals apart from primates that are known to use tools to get at their food.

The chimp's toolkit

Among wild primates, chimpanzees are the undisputed experts at making and using tools. In order to feed on ants and termites, a chimp searches for a flexible twig and strips it of its bark. The chimp then inserts the twig into a hole in an ant or termite nest and waits for the insects to start crawling up it. With a deft movement, the chimp sweeps them off with its mouth, like someone licking up the last traces of an ice cream. Without the twig, eating small insects would take too much energy to be worthwhile; with it, the chimp gets a mouthful of insects at a time. Chimps also smash open nuts with stones, and they use leaves to wipe their fur. They even use sticks and stones as weapons – something eerily reminiscent of the way that human ancestors would have behaved over 2 million years ago.

SEAFOOD SPECIALIST Floating on its back, a sea otter uses a stone to smash open its catch. Sea otters pick their stones carefully, choosing ones that are round and flat, and they may keep the same one for several days.

Chimps are born with instinctive curiosity, and also a talent for copying what they see. This copy-cat behaviour helps to maintain the different toolmaking traditions that are found in separate chimp groups. A chimp's long childhood helps it to develop its skills in just the same way that we develop ours.

Secret talents

In captivity, the two other great apes – orang utans and gorillas – can be remarkably playful and inventive. At an orang utan rescue centre in Borneo, one animal even untied a boat and successfully cast off, having watched to see how it was done. But neither of these two primates was thought to use tools in the wild, until some fascinating discoveries in recent years turned this idea on its head.

Orang utans are normally solitary animals, which means that they have little opportunity to learn skills from each other. But in the early 1990s, researchers found an isolated area of Sumatra where dozens of the animals were living in almost daily contact. These orang utans used sticks to extract seeds from spiky fruit – a form of behaviour that had never been observed before. The entire group had this toolmaking skill, even though nearby orang utans, on the opposite bank of a large river, showed no signs of toolmaking at all. As with chimps, 'copy cat' behaviour seems to have helped toolmaking to spread. But because orang utans cannot cross deep water, the skill never spread to the other side of the river.

HIT OR MISS The Egyptian vulture's egg-smashing technique has probably been 'invented' more than once, by birds living at different times and in different places. Copying keeps the skill alive.

This find was followed by an even more astonishing one in 2005. Workers in a national park in Central Africa filmed a female gorilla wading into a murky pond, using a stick to test the water's depth. This was a rare example of an animal using a tool for something other than collecting food. It meant that the gorilla had analysed the problem in an abstract way, before selecting a stick that was long enough for the job. It also had to understand how to use the stick – a double first for an animal that was once thought to be the slowest-witted of all the great apes.

MEET

ING 6

TWINING THEIR TRUNKS, TWO YOUNG BULL ELEPHANTS ENGAGE IN A FRIENDLY TUSSLE IN THE AFRICAN BUSH. For elephants, meetings are always important occasions, whether they involve animals catching up with their herd, or relatives who have not seen each other for months – relatives greet each other with huge excitement, while strangers get a guarded reception. This kind of affection is extremely rare in nature. Even so, few animals completely ignore their own kind. Encounters are almost inevitable, although instinct drives them to relate to one another in different ways. Some, such as wolves, live their whole lives together in packs with strict hierarchies; others, such as tigers, come together only to mate. Sometimes, different instincts in the same animal clash, leading to 'displacement behaviour' – behaviour that seems irrelevant or oddly out of place.

ANIMAL ENCOUNTERS

STAND-OFF Standing literally face to face, two black rhinos meet at the boundary of their territories. Their front horns can grow up to 1.2 m long and are formidable weapons, but rhinos rarely use them on each other.

SOME ANIMALS ARE MORE SOCIAL THAN OTHERS, BUT ON LAND VERY FEW SPEND THEIR ENTIRE LIVES ON THEIR OWN. Meetings with others of their kind are inevitable, whether as brief contacts dozens of times a day or occasional stand-offs.
For solitary creatures, such as black rhinos, these meetings tend to be tense affairs, especially if one animal has intruded into another's territory.

Black rhinos are placid enough when they meet in the neutral zone of a waterhole, but on home ground a different set of rules applies. Males greet females by snorting and lowering their horns, although they quickly give way if the female ignores them and carries on. With neighbouring males a quick 'identity check' is usually enough, as the two animals come up close to each other to confirm their familiar smells. If the intruder comes from further afield, however, the resident male confronts the other by crossing horns. At this point, rhino etiquette demands that the intruder withdraws. But he must do so quietly. If he makes the mistake of running away, the territory owner sets off in hot pursuit, charging across the savannah at up to 50 km/h – an impressive turn of speed for an animal that can weigh over a tonne.

Rhino etiquette demands that a male intruding on another male's territory withdraws. But he must do so quietly. If he makes the mistake of running away, the territory owner sets off in hot pursuit, charging across the savannah at up to 50 km/h.

Sending a signal
Rhinos are short-sighted, and their one-to-one encounters are dominated by smell. When tigers meet, the visual signals of body language play a much more important role. A tiger's facial expression shows if it is being assertive or submissive – a very important difference, because over-assertive intruders run the risk of being attacked

*CLOSE CONTACT For adult tigers, this
kind of intimacy is a rare event. Instinct
normally keeps tigers apart, except during
the breeding season when the male and
female briefly stay together.*

and killed. Scent also plays its part with tigers.
Normally, the only time adult tigers stay together
is when they mate and that lasts for just a few
days. For the rest of the time, they are secretive
and solitary, leaving few visible signs of their
existence, apart from their tracks on the ground
and the scarred bark of trees where they have
sharpened their claws.

Yet despite this aloofness, they are usually
well aware of their neighbours' movements, thanks
to a communication system based on scent. In
their natural habitat of forest and tall grassland,
tigers often leave scent marks as they search for food.
This means that when neighbours do meet, they will probably
tolerate each other since they have already been 'introduced' by
smell. If a tiger dies and its territory becomes vacant, its scent
signature soon begins to fade, giving the green light for another
tiger to take its place.

This, at least, is tigers' natural behaviour in the few places
where they are still numerous enough to stay in contact with one
another. In zoos, tigers are often much more sociable,
particularly if they are members of the same
family. Deep down, however, all tigers are
solitary animals, with a carnivore's
predatory instincts and awesome

killing power. After years of docile behaviour, these instincts
can be triggered without warning, even in a zoo, making a tiger
unleash a potentially fatal attack.

Relatives in town

Life could hardly be more different for prairie dogs – not, in fact,
dogs at all, but rodents of the North American grasslands that
burrow in systems called 'towns'. Today, prairie dog towns are
rarely more than 10 km across. But before the grasslands were
ploughed up for agriculture, one of the largest towns, in Texas,
covered 60 000 km² – nearly a tenth of the state. This colossal
network of burrows housed some 400 million animals, making
it the largest single colony of mammals on Earth.

*SEALED WITH A KISS With a quick
peck on the mouth, two prairie dogs in
Montana exchange a friendly
greeting. Prairie dogs recognise
close relatives chiefly by smell, so
a kiss is an ideal way of keeping
an extended family together.*

Each prairie dog town is divided into neighbourhoods called 'wards'. These are home to dozens or even hundreds of family groups, known as 'coteries'. When members of the same coterie meet, they often 'kiss' – a nose-to-nose greeting that involves touching teeth, sometimes producing a clicking sound. This ritual helps prairie dogs to recognise their kin from the hundreds of others in their ward. Outsiders from other parts of the town are often ejected.

Among other rodents, many recognise each other by scent. For example, when brown rats meet, they know each other's sex, age and family history, simply on the basis of their smell – this is a useful identity system in the dark. Recognition does not necessarily lead to friendliness, however. Resident rats will repel foreign-smelling intruders – an instinct that helps them to keep their food supplies to themselves.

Invader ants and impostors

Ants are legendary for being always on the move. But when two worker ants meet head-on, they stop for an instant to carry out a quick identity check. If they come from the same nest, their smell is identical and they let each other pass. But if one is an outsider, the other immediately releases a chemical messenger, or pheromone, which sounds the alarm, triggering defensive action.

Ants have good reason to behave like this, because their worst enemies include other ants. Given a chance, slave-making ants will force their way into a nest and carry away the eggs and developing grubs. Once installed in the slave-makers' nest, these young ants grow up as full-time slaves. Alternatively, the slave-makers may take over a nest by introducing their own queen,

who kills the rightful occupant, allowing the slave-makers to take control. Because worker ants are practically blind, other strangers, too, manage to slip past them, using chemical and other disguises. These include harmless animals, such as woodlice, as well as voracious predators, such as the caterpillars of the large blue butterfly (see opposite), which secrete a liquid attractive to the ants and are also able to mimic the shape of ant grubs.

FOOD ON THE MOVE Dwarfed by pieces of foliage, leafcutter ants head back to their nest. These workers are protected by soldiers, who move up and down the line, checking for intruders.

LARGE BLUE

THE LARGE BLUE BUTTERFLY HAS A BIZARRE LIFE HISTORY, WHICH INVOLVES BEING 'ADOPTED' BY ANTS. Despite its name, the large blue is less than 2 cm long, and its caterpillar is even tinier, looking like a pale yellow grub. The caterpillar starts life feeding on flowers, but after growing and shedding its skin several times, its lifestyle changes in a sudden and dramatic way. The details were discovered in 1915, when an English butterfly expert spotted a small ant picking up a caterpillar and carrying it back to its nest. He found that instead of eating the caterpillar, the ants are fooled by its smell and shape. The caterpillar first of all attracts the ants by secreting a sweet liquid, which they like to feed on. Then the caterpillar inflates the skin behind its head, giving it the shape of an ant grub, which triggers the ants' protective instincts. They treat it as one of their own grubs, placing it in their underground nursery and looking after it while it grows.

Once the caterpillar is underground, it becomes something like a cuckoo in the nest. It changes into a predator, with a rapacious appetite for ant grubs. By the time it is fully grown at the beginning of spring, it may have eaten as many as a thousand grubs. At this point, the caterpillar turns into a chrysalis. A few weeks later, the adult butterfly emerges and crawls out of the ants' nest, then it unfolds its wings and flies away. This remarkable lifestyle has evolved among several closely related blue butterflies, but most of them use ants' nests simply as a safe place to hibernate. The large blue is one of the few that goes further, by plundering its underground refuge.

VITAL STATISTICS

CLASS: Insects
ORDER: Lepidoptera
SPECIES: *Maculinea arion*
HABITAT: Grassland
DISTRIBUTION: Europe, Russia, China and Japan
KEY FEATURE: Caterpillar is carnivorous, feeding on ant grubs

KNOWING
YOUR PLACE

LOPING ACROSS A FROZEN LAKE, A PACK OF WOLVES SEEMS TO EPITOMISE THE FREEDOM OF LIFE IN THE WILD. But for wolves, freedom is not quite what it appears. In a wolf pack, every animal knows its place in the hierarchy and will be punished if it oversteps the mark.

After centuries of persecution, wolves have been driven from most of the places that were once their homes. But in the far north of North America, Europe and Asia and in some remote parts of central Asia – often on the very edge of survival – wolf packs still roam with little interference from man. A typical pack is an extended family, containing up to a dozen members. Half of them may be fully grown, but only two adults, known as the 'alpha pair', actually breed. They mate for life, and one of them – normally the male – is leader of the pack.

Within the pack, the leader combines the roles of military tactician and chief of law enforcement. He decides when the pack will set off on a hunt and which part of its

BROUGHT INTO LINE An alpha male shows his authority to a junior pack member, who cowers and licks his nose in a gesture of appeasement.

LONG-DISTANCE RUNNERS Grey wolves run across the winter snow in the Rocky Mountains of North America. Their equal spacing is typical of wolf packs on the move.

territory they will target. On rare occasions – if they are after bison, for example – the leader will sanction a temporary alliance with a neighbouring pack, so that the wolves can work together to bring down their prey. As leader, he will be at the head of the chase, a position he also occupies if the pack is under threat. Beneath him, the chain of command runs downwards, reinforced by the complex body language used when wolves interact.

Called to order

For a wolf expert, it takes just a few minutes' close observation to work out who is in charge. The pack leader bares his teeth at troublesome subordinates, while a junior wolf shows its submission by lowering its tail and licking the leader's nose. If a subordinate wolf has been involved in a fight, the leader steps in and restores order. The troublemaker often shrinks back and drops on its haunches or lies down on its side. Both postures are familiar to dog owners, which is not surprising, because dogs have inherited these instincts directly from wolves – domestic dogs almost certainly originated as domesticated wolves and have changed very little in the last 10 000 years.

Below the rank of leader, less senior wolves show their status in exactly the same way. Each wolf dominates the ones below it, ending with the youngest subadults – normally the previous year's pups. Recently born pups acquire their rank early on, by play-fighting with their peers. As they grow up, they rise from rank to rank, until finally they may leave the pack to start a new one of their own. For the leader, staying at the top depends on physical fitness. When that fails and the leader dies, the strict hierarchy means that another leader is ready to take its place.

CHAIN OF COMMAND

In a typical wolf pack, the chain of command starts with the alpha male and extends downwards to juveniles. Young cubs do not develop a rank until they have been weaned.

1 Alpha male
The leader of the pack, and the only male that breeds. Alpha males remain at the head of the pack until they die or become so weak that one of their young can oust them.

2 Alpha female
The dominant female, and the only one that breeds. All the subadults, juveniles and cubs are her young. Alpha females occasionally lead the pack.

3 Subadults
Typical number: 2-3. At two years old, these are ready to breed. They do so only if they leave the pack, or if one of the alpha pair dies or is overthrown.

4 Juveniles
Typical number: 3-4. At one year old, these take part in hunts but are not sexually mature.

5 Cubs
Typical number: 4-8. Offspring of the alpha pair, these are looked after by their parents, the subadults and the juveniles.

MAKING UP

IN THE HUMAN WORLD, AGGRESSIVE BEHAVIOUR CAN ALL TOO EASILY SPIRAL OUT OF CONTROL. But in the wild, our closest relatives, the other primates, have tried-and-tested ways of defusing conflict before serious damage is done. These conflict-resolution techniques are of growing interest to behavioural scientists, although some of the methods used would undoubtedlly cause consternation if we tried them out ourselves. One startling strategy – used by macaques and baboons – could be called 'snatch the baby'. More a defensive trick than a proper burying of the hatchet, it involves grabbing an infant and using it like a shield. Infants arouse strong protective instincts in most primates, so holding onto a young one will usually defuse

CAUGHT IN THE MIDDLE This young Barbary macaque is being held hostage during a dispute between two adults.

TENDER TOUCH Two orphaned chimps comfort each other with a mouth-to-mouth embrace. Like humans, apes and monkeys have an instinctive need for physical contact – if deprived of it by losing their mother, they often seek it from others of their own age.

a possible attack by an aggressor. As a tactic, it does have a downside: its effect quickly wears off when the baby is no longer there, so the argument can begin again.

With many conflicts – among both humans and wild primates – it soon becomes clear who is on the winning side. At this point, however, a difficult situation can set in, because the loser, even though it knows it is losing, cannot stop until it is assured that it will able to back away without being harmed. Baboons have their own way of tackling this situation: the loser switches to food-begging behaviour, which again triggers off protective instincts in its opponents, allowing it to end the skirmish in a peaceful way.

Once a dispute has been brought to an end, further peacekeeping behaviour is needed between the winner and the loser, so that hostilities do not break out again. Many primates do this by mutual grooming – behaviour that has both a practical use and symbolic value at the same time.

Reconciliation and mediation

Chimps live in 'fission-fusion' societies. These are based on communities of up to 100 animals, within which chimps live and forage in much smaller bands that are hardly ever all in the same place at the same time.

Relations within the bands, and even between different bands in the same community, are generally amicable, though fights can break out from time to time – particularly between males. However, relations between neighbouring communities are far more hostile and are often described as being like those between warring human tribes. When chimps from different communities meet, there are no attempts at peacemaking and in the fighting that follows, neither side shows any mercy.

The same animals behave very differently on the occasions when they have disputes among their own community. Like many humans, chimps seem to recognise when a quarrel has gone on for too long and it is time to bring it to an end. Two rivals will suddenly break off fighting and cautiously approach each other for a public embrace. If that goes well, they often seal their new understanding with a kiss.

Sometimes the strain of embracing a former rival proves too much and the fighting suddenly breaks out all over again. If this happens, only time will defuse the conflict, unless a mediator intervenes. This remarkable behaviour – which has been spotted only occasionally by chimp researchers – usually involves a senior chimp, such as an old female, who brings the two opponents together, helping to bring a halt to the squabble between them, rather like a human teacher dealing with two fighting children.

Free-loving bonobos

The chimpanzee's smaller and lesser-known relative, the bonobo, also lives in communities, but its social life is very different. Bonobos are instinctively tolerant, and their communities often share overlapping ground. Animals from neighbouring communities usually avoid each other, but if they do come into contact, there is none of the open warfare seen in their bigger relatives. Encounters can be noisy, with threatening displays and occasionally actual fights, but most of the confrontation is for show. Once it has run its course, the bonobos get on with the more important business of finding food, which for them, unlike chimps, consists mainly of fruit and plant stems.

Peacemaking among bonobos is carried out in a remarkable way, which took some time to make it into scientific reports. The reason was embarrassment, because bonobos use sex to calm ruffled feelings. In a bonobo community, sex oils the wheels of social contact, and bonobos indulge in it frequently, openly and in many different ways. This 'free love' lifestyle is extremely unusual for any animal, particularly when it is not directly connected with reproduction. Bonobos treat sex as a way of repaying favours and of defusing tension before serious trouble has a chance to start.

INNER CONFLICT

WHEN COMPUTERS RUN SEVERAL PROGRAMS AT ONCE, IT IS NOT UNUSUAL FOR ONE TO CONFLICT WITH ANOTHER. Something similar can happen with animals, when two or more instincts try to make them behave in different ways. An everyday example of this inner conflict happens with domestic dogs. Confronted by a stranger on the edge of their territory, many dogs will rush towards the intruder, baring their teeth and barking in an aggressive way. But when the dog gets near to the person, it often backs off with its tail between its legs. Seconds later, it goes on the offensive again, and the cycle continues until the stranger is out of sight.

This seesawing behaviour is produced by two instincts that are literally driving the dog in opposite directions. The first instinct is the one that makes the dog defend its territory – something inherited from its wild ancestor, the wolf. The second, also inherited from the wolf, is a fear reaction of being on 'foreign' territory belonging to a different pack. One instinct drives the dog forwards, but as it nears the edge of its territory, the retreat instinct grows and eventually drives it back. The dog runs backwards and forwards, until the stranger has finally gone away.

Instead of seesawing back and forth, conflicting instincts sometimes make animals combine different types of behaviour into a type of halfway house. For example, if a duck is offered food, it will often clamber out of the water to take it, but then as it cranes forwards, it may suddenly turn its body away. Seeing the food,

WHO DARES WINS Aggression and fear are finely balanced as these dingos squabble over the carcass of a dead kangaroo. The dingo on the left is on the defensive, as the one on the right tries to prevent it from pushing in.

the duck gets out of the water, but fear prevents it from eating. The duck is temporarily trapped in an 'ambivalent posture' – a compromise between two different instincts: the instinct to feed and the instinct to steer clear of large animals.

Displacement activities

If two computer programs clash, a human operator eventually has to sort them out, but animals do not have this kind of technical backup, so evolution has given them different ways of dealing with their own internal 'software clashes'. One of the commonest is displacement behaviour, when an animal plunges into an everyday activity that in the circumstances looks oddly irrelevant or out of place.

For example, when birds are raising their young, they spend a lot of time collecting food. If a parent flies back and finds a predator nearby, instead of either approaching its nest or flying away, it will often settle on a branch and start preening its feathers. To a human eye, preening seems an odd way to respond to this apparently dangerous situation, but it is something that many birds do when their instincts conflict – in this case, the instinct to look after their young and the instinct to avoid danger. In the bird world, displacement activities include many everyday routines, such as beak-wiping, scratching and pulling up pieces of

TIME OUT Like mirror images of each other, these two goosanders are preening their feathers. Preening is a common kind of displacement behaviour.

grass. Each is a perfectly normal piece of behaviour, but it seems to be carried out at an inappropriate time. Mammals, too, have their own kind of displacement behaviour, which works in a similar way. When two cats fight, one may break off suddenly and begin grooming its fur, as if it had nothing more pressing to do. Humans do it as well. In tense business meetings, we stroke our chins, scratch behind our ears and fiddle with all kinds of inanimate objects from pencils to mobile phones.

Taking off the brake

What exactly is happening when animals do this? Since the early days of behavioural science, researchers have been fascinated by displacement behaviour in animals and have put forward various hypotheses to try to explain it. Dutch biologist Nikolaas Tinbergen, one of the first and most famous specialists in the field (who won the Nobel prize for physiology or medicine in 1973), suggested that it was a way of dissipating pent-up nervous energy. This spilled over when an instinct was blocked, triggering another instinct that was out of place.

Today, most scientists prefer the idea that instincts compete with each other, like runners in a race. At any given moment, one instinct has the lead. It gets top priority, controlling what the animal does. But if another instinct comes to the fore, it is as if the former leader has pulled out of the race, while the new leader dictates behaviour. This more up-to-date explanation of displacement activities means that they may not be quite as irrelevant as at first they seem. It could explain, for example, the displacement behaviour seen in sticklebacks. These small fish are highly territorial, and when neighbouring males meet, one of them will often swim head-down and dig up sand with its mouth. This is exactly what sticklebacks do when they build their nests. In stickleback body language, this 'inappropriate behaviour' may actually spell out: Private Property – Keep Out.

HOW BEHAVIOUR EVOLVES

YOU SCRATCH MY NECK... Horses groom their coats with their teeth, but they cannot reach their own shoulders and necks. These wild horses in Mongolia show how group evolution has come up with a solution to the problem.

WHEN PEOPLE THINK ABOUT EVOLUTION, BONES AND FOSSILS OFTEN COME FIRST TO MIND. But evolution shapes everything that is controlled by genes and passed on when parents breed. That includes instinct – something that does not show up in fossils, meaning that scientists have no firm evidence about instincts in the past. But like all forms of behaviour, instinct is likely to have evolved in small steps, each of which gave different animals a better chance of survival. The result – millions of years later – is the amazing variety of instinctive behaviour in the animal world today.

Simple activities, like keeping clean, must have evolved early on in the story of animal life, since animals cannot function properly if their mouthparts and other important organs are clogged by dirt. So when a housefly cleans its wings, it is using instincts that date back to the very first true flies, which appeared during the Permian period over 245 million years ago. During that immense interval of time, flies and their instincts have evolved hand in hand.

For birds and mammals, keeping clean is even more important. Because they are warm-blooded and covered by an insulating jacket of feathers or fur, they must keep this protective layer in good condition in order to retain their body heat. A bird's preening instincts were inherited from its reptilian ancestors – small feathered dinosaurs, which eventually evolved the ability to fly. These dinosaurs probably preened their body feathers by 'combing' them with their teeth. Birds no longer have teeth, but they have beaks, which they use instead, smoothing out their feathers and keeping them waterproof by smearing them with oil.

All birds and mammals groom themselves, but some also groom each other. Parrots preen their partners' feathers, while horses often stand in pairs, facing opposite ways, so that each can groom the neck of the other. This helps horses to groom parts of their bodies they cannot reach themselves. In apes and monkeys, evolution has gone further by turning mutual grooming into a social activity, which helps to reduce tension and reinforce bonds. During primate evolution, the instinct for grooming has become 'ritualised', giving it a new and special significance.

The birth of a ritual

Ritualisation has happened time and again during animal evolution. All kinds of behaviour, from keeping clean to finding food, can develop into rituals, each of which means something different. When an activity becomes ritualised, it often evolves in a way that makes it distinct from other kinds of behaviour and easy for animals to recognise. For example, when chimps groom each other, the way they do it is different from the way in which they groom themselves. In ritual grooming, the groomer concentrates only on certain parts of the body.

With woodpeckers, the pecking behaviour used to get at food has evolved into several different rituals. One of these is the male woodpecker's 'call sign' – a ritual burst of hammering at a precise rate, which reverberates around woodlands in spring. Each species of woodpecker has its own hammering pattern, which is quite unlike the irregular pecking it uses when it feeds. Once a woodpecker has attracted a female, another pecking ritual appears, which partners use during incubation to tell each other when they are ready for their turn to sit on the nest.

Behavioural family trees

Because instinct evolves, it should be possible to use it like any other inherited feature to piece together animal family trees. So grooming rituals, say, could be used to work out the evolution of primates, while different ways of raising a family could be used to chart the evolution of frogs. Scientists have tried this method of 'winding back the clock' by looking at the behaviour of different groups of birds. For

NOW HEAR THIS Like all woodpeckers, the northern flicker has its own distinctive call sign. It hammers its beak against tree trunks, even though it gets most of its food on the ground.

example, cormorants and their relatives – which include gannets and darters – display to their partners by pointing their heads skywards or flapping their wings. Some species wave their wings rapidly, while others are much slower. Darters, or anhingas, are unique because they flap one wing at a time. Experts think it is likely that all these ritual movements evolved from behaviour that birds normally use just before they take off.

By comparing all these displays, researchers have drawn up a family tree that puts similar displays together and differing ones further apart. This 'behavioural' tree can then be compared with a traditional one, which is based on physical features and differences in genes. The results are fascinating and clear-cut: the two trees largely agree, showing that bird's 'software' or instincts evolve hand in hand with their 'hardware', such as beaks and bones.

ANIMAL
LANGUA

GE7

WHEN A PROBOSCIS MONKEY CALLS THROUGH THE TREETOPS, ITS MESSAGE IS LOUD AND CLEAR. Its call – a deep *kee-honk* – echoes through its home in a mangrove forest, telling other proboscis monkeys exactly where it is. Like many animals, it is born with an instinct to communicate, something that existed long before humans developed spoken words. Animal language is about passing on information, and it does not always rely on sound. Animals also use colours, movements or even chemical signals to get their message across. Animal language holds a powerful fascination, particularly when it sheds light on the way we communicate ourselves. After decades of research with chimps and other primates, scientists have been able to realise an age-old dream: that of communicating directly with animals and finding out what they have to say.

COMMUNICATE

In the animal world, communication between different species is the exception rather than the rule.

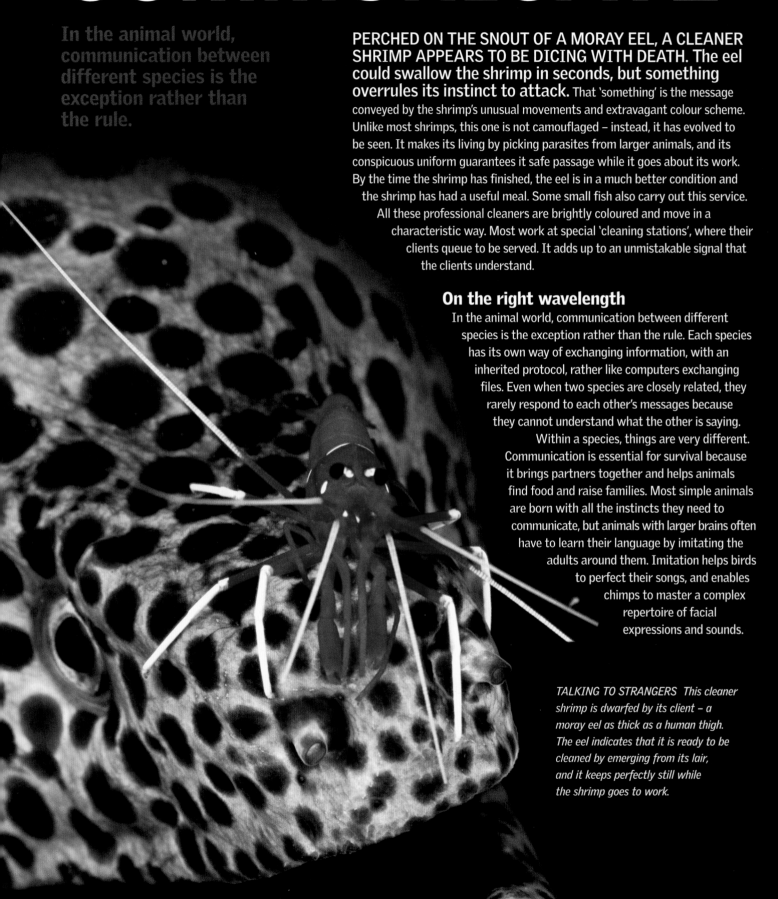

PERCHED ON THE SNOUT OF A MORAY EEL, A CLEANER SHRIMP APPEARS TO BE DICING WITH DEATH. The eel could swallow the shrimp in seconds, but something overrules its instinct to attack. That 'something' is the message conveyed by the shrimp's unusual movements and extravagant colour scheme. Unlike most shrimps, this one is not camouflaged – instead, it has evolved to be seen. It makes its living by picking parasites from larger animals, and its conspicuous uniform guarantees it safe passage while it goes about its work. By the time the shrimp has finished, the eel is in a much better condition and the shrimp has had a useful meal. Some small fish also carry out this service. All these professional cleaners are brightly coloured and move in a characteristic way. Most work at special 'cleaning stations', where their clients queue to be served. It adds up to an unmistakable signal that the clients understand.

On the right wavelength

In the animal world, communication between different species is the exception rather than the rule. Each species has its own way of exchanging information, with an inherited protocol, rather like computers exchanging files. Even when two species are closely related, they rarely respond to each other's messages because they cannot understand what the other is saying. Within a species, things are very different. Communication is essential for survival because it brings partners together and helps animals find food and raise families. Most simple animals are born with all the instincts they need to communicate, but animals with larger brains often have to learn their language by imitating the adults around them. Imitation helps birds to perfect their songs, and enables chimps to master a complex repertoire of facial expressions and sounds.

TALKING TO STRANGERS This cleaner shrimp is dwarfed by its client – a moray eel as thick as a human thigh. The eel indicates that it is ready to be cleaned by emerging from its lair, and it keeps perfectly still while the shrimp goes to work.

DANCING IN THE DARK

DESPITE HAVING TINY BRAINS, HONEYBEES USE ONE OF THE MOST COMPLEX LANGUAGES IN THE ANIMAL WORLD. By dancing in the depths of its hive, a worker bee can tell its colleagues where it has just found food. Honeybee dances were decoded by the Austrian zoologist, Karl von Frisch, in 1945. At the time, his findings met with astonishment bordering on disbelief, but since then, scientists have confirmed that he was right: honeybees pass on detailed information by dancing in the dark.

The dance begins when a female worker bee returns from a successful foraging trip. She makes her way onto the vertical surface of the honeycomb, where she is surrounded by other workers, who follow her as she starts to move. If the food is less than 25 m from the hive, she performs the 'round dance', moving in a circle across the comb. As she dances she keeps changing direction, and the more often she does this, the better the food. Acting on this information, her fellow workers set off and soon track down the food that she has found.

If the food is further away, the bee performs the 'waggle dance'. This time, she moves over the surface of the honeycomb in a figure-of-eight, waggling her abdomen as she completes the section linking the two loops. The rate of waggling shows how far the bees have to fly, while the line's angle to the vertical shows the direction they must take, using the Sun as their reference point. The dancing bee even takes account of the time, adjusting the angle of its dance as the day wears on and the Sun moves across the sky.

Family instincts

How did these extraordinary dancing instincts evolve? To find out, researchers have looked at the honeybee's wild relatives, which all come from South-east Asia, like the honeybee itself. One of these bees builds nests with a single honeycomb hanging in the open air. The top of the honeycomb has a flat platform, which the bees use when they land. When one of these bees finds food, it lands on the platform and carries out a dance that points towards the food. The message to the other workers is simple: to find food, follow this line.

Another kind of bee also builds its honeycombs in the open, but dances on the combs. Instead of pointing towards the food, it makes a symbolic leap by showing the food's position compared with that of the Sun. This is very similar to the system used by the honeybee, although honeybees nest in dark cavities and have to communicate by touch. Because all these bees share the same distant ancestor, it is likely that the honeybee dance developed through similar stages to those of species with open-air combs, millions of years ago.

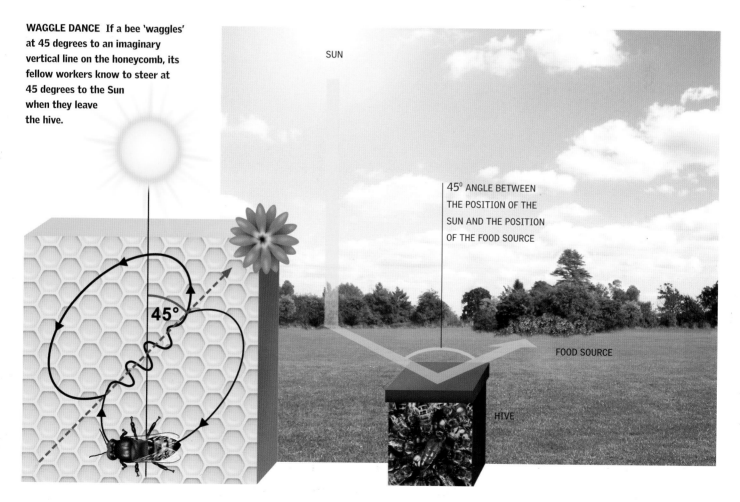

WAGGLE DANCE If a bee 'waggles' at 45 degrees to an imaginary vertical line on the honeycomb, its fellow workers know to steer at 45 degrees to the Sun when they leave the hive.

SUN

45° ANGLE BETWEEN THE POSITION OF THE SUN AND THE POSITION OF THE FOOD SOURCE

45°

FOOD SOURCE

HIVE

CHEMICAL COMMUNICATION

SCENT MARKS Using a gland near its eye, a male Thomson's gazelle marks a plant with its oily scent to define the boundary of its territory. Like all the best perfumes, the scent evaporates very slowly, ensuring that it lingers for several days.

IN THE HUMAN BRAIN, THE PART THAT DEALS WITH SMELL IS TINY COMPARED TO THE PARTS THAT PROCESS SIGHTS AND SOUNDS. In many animals the opposite is true, allowing them to use chemicals for communication. These message-carrying substances are called semiochemicals, and animals make and release them at particular times. They are often released in tiny amounts, but can have dramatic and far-reaching effects.

The number of chemical signals in the animal world runs into hundreds of thousands. Most pass us by, but animals pick them up all the time, especially the ones that warn would-be predators to keep away. Some are like radio messages broadcast on many frequencies, so they are easily received and understood by other species. Most chemical communication is more focused than this. Instead of broadcasting public messages, many animals communicate on their own private channels, using chemicals called pheromones.

When an antelope marks a plant by rubbing it with scent, it leaves a pheromone message that lasts for several days. Pheromones are chemicals that one animal makes to trigger off behaviour in another. They are sometimes passed on by direct contact, but more often animals release them into the air, or leave them behind on plants or other objects as they move about. An antelope marks plants with pheromones by using scent glands near its eyes. The scent tells other antelopes all about it without the sender and recipient having to meet. Antelopes also make pheromones in glands above each hoof and leave a trail wherever they roam. This works like an identification badge; more importantly, it helps stray animals find their way back to the herd. At breeding time, antelopes use yet another set of pheromones as sex attractants. The great advantage of this communication system is that it is completely secure: most pheromone messages are specific to just one species and have no effect on anything else.

Social insects, such as bees and ants, communicate almost entirely by smell. For them, pheromones are as vital as words are for us. In a honeybee hive, the queen makes the most important pheromone of all. Called queen mandibular pheromone, or QMP, it signals that she is present. The queen produces QMP in her mandibles, or jaws, and the workers pass it on as they share food. This pheromone shuts down each worker's reproductive system so that they can devote all their time to tending the queen, raising her young and finding food. If the queen dies, the supply of QMP stops. The workers quickly sense this and respond by feeding royal jelly, a special substance secreted by the workers, to some of the grubs. These grubs develop into queens, and one eventually takes charge of the nest. In addition, each hive has its own chemical signature, which helps bees to return to the right hive. If they make a mistake, they risk being killed.

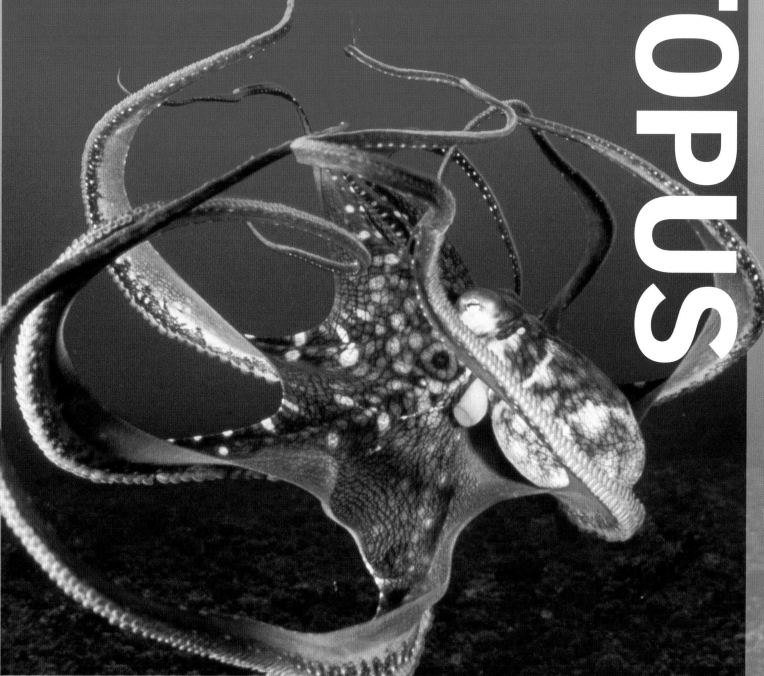

THE MOST INTELLIGENT INVERTEBRATES

IN THE WORLD, OCTOPUSES COMMUNICATE USING THEIR ENTIRE BODY, changing shape and colour, and even the texture of their skin. Unlike other invertebrates, octopuses are extremely expressive, and many researchers are convinced that they show emotions, ranging from interest and excitement to annoyance and even boredom. When octopuses meet, their body language depends on the other's sex. Males often darken when they meet other males, to make themselves look threatening, but females trigger a lighter colour. If a male octopus is placed between a male and a female, it can switch on different colours and patterns on opposite sides of its body, sending out two different signals at the same time.

There are nearly 300 species of octopus, and most live in shallow water close to coasts or on coral reefs. The day octopus (below) is one of the few species that is active in bright sunlight. When it is hunting, it constantly changes colour and pattern to match the dappled light and shadow on the seabed.

VITAL STATISTICS

CLASS: Cephalopoda

ORDER: Octopoda

SPECIES: *Octopus cyanea*

HABITAT: Seabed and coral reefs

DISTRIBUTION: Indian and
Pacific oceans

KEY FEATURES: Diurnal octopus
noted for its rapid and frequent
colour changes

BODY LANGUAGE

WHEN A WILD CAT ARCHES ITS BACK, FLATTENS ITS EARS AND HISSES, THERE IS LITTLE DOUBT WHAT IT MEANS. But what is a chimp saying when it flashes a toothy grin? The answer is all to do with body language – a communication system that is used throughout the animal world. Like many kinds of behaviour, basic body language is controlled by instinct, but its finer points often have to be learned. A wild cat's threat display is at one end of the spectrum: it is 100 per cent instinctive, which is why kittens use it when they are just a few days old. Similar behaviour runs throughout the cat family, and the message comes across loud and clear, in a way that other animals can easily understand.

Chimp facial expressions are far more complex than the body language used by cats. Chimps make some of these expressions by instinct, but they learn many of them as they grow up. Altogether, researchers have found over 20, indicating a wide range of feelings from aggression or playfulness to fear. Some expressions vary subtly between different chimp populations, in the same way as a regional accent. But unlike a cat's threat display, chimp facial expressions are highly specific, and most can only be understood by chimps themselves. Even we find them difficult to grasp: what looks to us like a happy grin is actually a chimp's way of showing subservience and fear.

'See what I mean'

For animals, being able to make faces is an unusual skill, and primates lead the field in this kind of body language. Most animal faces are expressionless – there is no such thing as a frowning fish or a smiling frog. Instead, their body language is often based on the way they hold themselves. Birds use this kind of communication just as much as they do sound. When starlings or gulls are squabbling over food, they will often extend their heads and bodies horizontally, with their beaks pointing towards any bird that tries to come too close. They take this stance when they are about to launch an attack on another bird, but in this ritual form it also works as a message, telling other birds to keep out of pecking distance. Birds also do the reverse of this action: in many species, such as storks and gannets, partners greet each other by pointing their beaks skywards, where they are safely out of the way. Body language gets particularly interesting in animals that can change colour, such as chameleons, octopuses, cuttlefish and squid. Chameleons change colour to match their background, but their most impressive displays are reserved for the rare occasions when they come face to face with other chameleons. Males often react to each other by turning darker, as if each one is infuriated to discover the other in its terrain. The change can take several minutes, but as chameleons move very slowly, there is plenty of time for the message to get across. Cuttlefish are much faster: in a split second they can switch on speckles or stripes, or make waves of colour sweep across their bodies and the single, wrap-around fin. In a tank the effect is hypnotic, giving the impression that their thoughts can be read simply by looking at their skin.

NAKED AGGRESSION The wild cat's threat display warns that it is primed to attack with teeth and needle-sharp claws.

FACIAL EXPRESSIONS IN CHIMPS

No other wild animal can match chimps for their richness of facial expressions. These expressions, which are a highly distilled form of body language, allow chimps to communicate all kinds of feelings and intentions, from playfulness to rage. Some expressions are purely visual, while others are backed up with sounds.

A DROOPING LOWER LIP SHOWS THIS CHIMP IS RELAXED

POUTING AND PANTING SHOW ENJOYMENT

BARED TEETH INDICATE FEAR OR THREATENING BEHAVIOUR

A BIG GRIN SHOWS EXCITEMENT DURING A HUNT

MESSAGES IN SOUND

BY THE AGE OF TWO, DOLPHINS HAVE THEIR OWN PERSONAL SIGNATURE, 'WRITTEN' IN A SHORT BURST OF SOUND. Born with an irrepressible instinct to communicate, their noisy language is one of the few known to rival our own. Dolphins have poor eyesight, and vision plays a relatively small part in their lives. Instead, they see their world with sound. They sense their surroundings by echolocation, the same system that is used by insect-eating bats. With echolocation, river dolphins find fish in water that is as cloudy as coffee, and captive dolphins can 'see' transparent plastic panels that are submerged in their tanks. If a panel contains an opening, a dolphin can swim straight through it without a moment's hesitation, even in total darkness.

A dolphin's echolocation works with high frequency sounds that are largely beyond the range of human hearing, but we can hear many of the sounds that dolphins use to communicate with each other – something dolphins share with many other toothed whales, such as the beluga. Researchers studying Risso's dolphins have found that they make seven separate kinds of vocal noises, including whistles, clicks, chirps, buzzes and grunts. They can produce some of these sounds simultaneously, and

SHARED SIGNALS Mirrored in the water's surface, a school of Atlantic spotted dolphins heads out to sea. By picking up each other's calls, the dolphins can quickly react to danger or home in on food.

they also show a marked 'local accent' that varies between groups, or pods. The largest member of the dolphin family is the orca, or killer whale, found in oceans worldwide. Groups of pods, called clans, develop distinctive dialects, so orcas from the Southern Ocean would probably have trouble understanding ones from the Arctic Ocean, in the rare event that they actually met.

A dolphin's whistled signature develops like a human one, by experiment and practice, until the final version emerges. Once acquired, it stays with a dolphin for life. Dolphins use signatures to identify each other, and to signal when they have become separated from their pod. Dolphins are great mimics, and they sometimes copy each others' signatures to attract attention, or just for fun. In captivity, they copy their trainers' whistles; dolphins at the Disney Epcot Center, in Florida, have even mastered short snatches of film theme music – a bizarre first for a non-human mammal.

The underwater Internet

Personal call signs are not unique to dolphins. Many other animals – such as seabirds – instantly recognise their partners by their calls alone. But the richness of dolphin calls means that they can say much more than 'Hi, it's me'. At present, scientists know very little about what information dolphins communicate in the wild, but it is quite likely that their rapid chatter can express how they feel as well as carrying messages about food and danger.

Another side of their sonic life is that they can listen in on each other's echolocation signals. This raises the fascinating possibility that dolphins can find out about their surroundings from each other, as well as by themselves. If this is true, the result could work like an underwater version of the Internet, with information being shared through independent hubs. Most dolphin pods contain just a handful of animals, restricting the spread of information. But in some dolphin species, hundreds or thousands of animals can gather in temporary 'superpods'. When this happens, the members of a superpod would form a vast communication network with a combined brainpower far in excess of anything found in the wild on dry land.

Dolphins are great mimics ... In captivity, they often copy their trainers' whistles, and dolphins at the Disney Epcot Center, in Florida, have even mastered short snatches of film theme music.

TALKING
TO US

Researchers noticed that he was making sounds under his breath while carrying out particular activities. Kanzi seems to have invented four completely new 'bonobo words', which he uses in particular situations.

SINCE TIME IMMEMORIAL PEOPLE HAVE TALKED TO ANIMALS, BUT UNTIL RECENTLY, THE CONVERSATION HAS BEEN ENTIRELY ONE-WAY. Chimps and gorillas cannot reply in words, but they can communicate to humans with symbols and signs. One of the earliest communication projects involved Washoe, a chimp that was raised in the USA during the 1960s. Washoe's trainers – Allen and Beatrice Gardner – decided not to try teaching Washoe to speak, because all previous experiments with speech had failed. Instead, they taught her American Sign Language, or ASL, a communication system designed for use by the deaf. Some ASL signs are easily understood by non-signers, but many are abstract symbols, as are words.

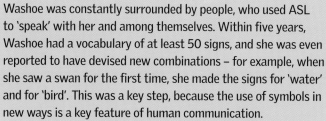

TWO-WAY COMMUNICATION Sitting with his trainer, Dr Sue Savage-Rumbaugh, Kanzi the bonobo spells out a message. He is using a visual keyboard specially designed for bonobos and chimpanzees.

Washoe was constantly surrounded by people, who used ASL to 'speak' with her and among themselves. Within five years, Washoe had a vocabulary of at least 50 signs, and she was even reported to have devised new combinations – for example, when she saw a swan for the first time, she made the signs for 'water' and for 'bird'. This was a key step, because the use of symbols in new ways is a key feature of human communication.

Despite this apparent breakthrough, scientists were divided about the project's results – and many still are today. Many linguists feel that Washoe's achievements fell far short of true language, and that what the project really showed was her copying skills, combined with the researchers' wishful thinking. However, such criticisms have not stopped the research. Since the 1960s, further language experiments have been carried out with chimps and gorillas, and with the chimp's closest relative, the pygmy chimp, or bonobo.

Koko the gorilla is the largest, and probably the most famous, of these signing primates. Raised by Dr Francine Patterson of Stanford University, Koko has been using ASL for over 30 years. She uses her own version of ASL, nicknamed GSL, its symbols being easier for an animal with big fingers and short thumbs. Koko's vocabulary runs to hundreds of signs, most of them for tangible objects, such as fruit. But she can also express abstract concepts. For example, she often uses the sign 'open' to show her carers when she wants to be let outside, instead of making the sign for a door.

Symbol stars

In recent years, some of the most remarkable breakthroughs in language research have come by abandoning signs in favour of keyboard symbols, known as lexigrams. Apes are taught to link lexigrams with spoken words, allowing them to use the keyboard to hold conversations.

A bonobo called Kanzi, who was born in 1980, amazed researchers by learning a number of symbols as an infant, when his mother was the 'pupil' being taught. His talent was spotted while his mother was away, and since then he has been at the centre of a long-term project into the way primates use language. As a youngster, Kanzi could make over 100 phrases using a 12-symbol keyboard. Today, he can understand about 500 words, even when they are spoken with different accents, or heard through headphones so that he cannot see the speaker moving their lips. He can use about 200 words himself on the keyboard, stringing them together in the correct order to make simple sentences. Now in middle age, his language skills are almost as good as a three-year-old child's.

Kanzi's progress continues to amaze his keepers. In 2003, researchers noticed that he was making sounds under his breath while carrying out particular activities. They recorded the sounds so that they could be studied. The results were remarkable. Kanzi seems to have invented four completely new 'bonobo words', which he uses in particular situations. This strange discovery makes Kanzi's keepers even more enthused by his skills.

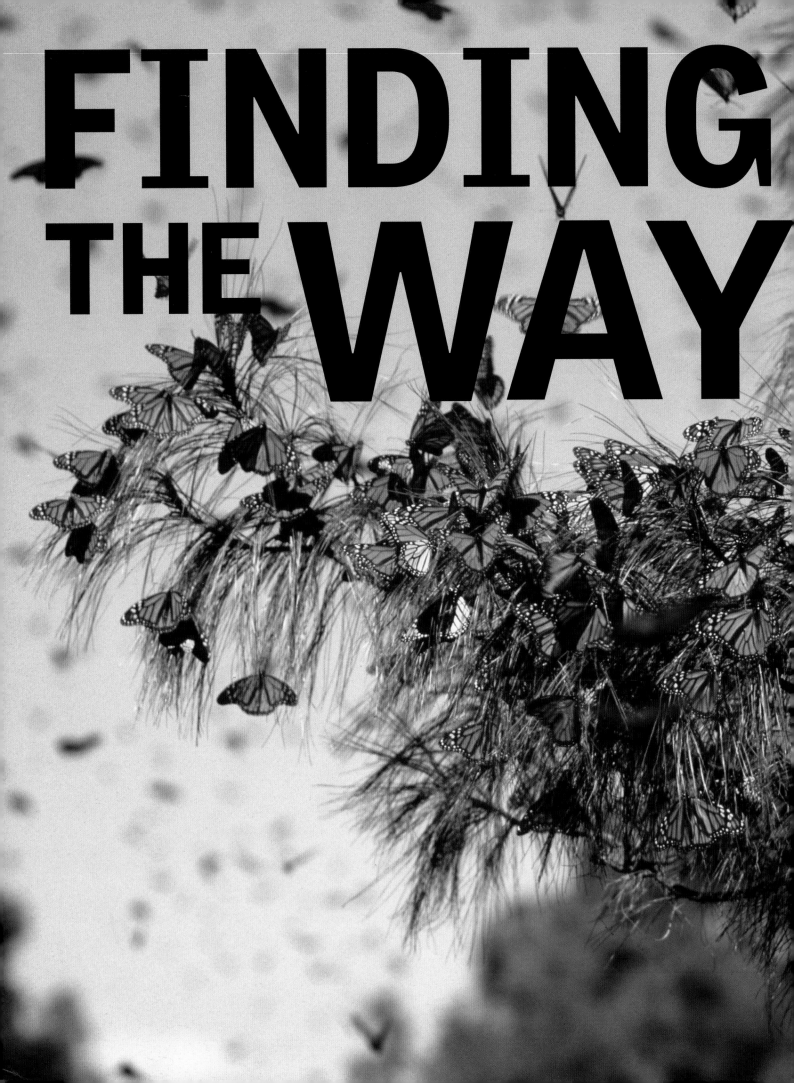

FINDING THE WAY

8

EVERY AUTUMN, MONARCH BUTTERFLIES IN NORTH AMERICA MAKE THEIR WAY SOUTHWARDS TO ESCAPE THE WINTER COLD. At first they travel in twos or threes, but soon millions gather in immense orange swarms. Monarchs to the west of the Rocky Mountains finish their journey in the warmth of California, where they spend the winter clustered on trees close to the coast. Ones to the east fly further – up to 3000 km – from Canada to the remote Mexican uplands of the Sierra Madre. Here they overwinter in pockets of pine forest, which scientists finally tracked down in 1975. Instinct guides them on this once-in-a-lifetime expedition, unique in the insect world, as it drives other animals on journeys as varied the desert ant's homeward trip after a busy day of foraging, to the Arctic tern's annual odyssey between the Arctic and the Antarctic.

ANIMALS AT HOME

HOMING IN When a digger wasp (left) flies back to its nest in the ground, it steers by looking for landmarks. If a circle of pinecones is put around its nest, the wasp uses them to navigate, and becomes confused if they are moved.

CIRCLE POSITIONED AROUND NEST

CIRCLE MOVED AWAY FROM NEST

NO MATTER HOW FAR ANIMALS TRAVEL, THEY NEED TO BE ABLE TO FIND THEIR WAY HOME. Thanks to a combination of instinct and learning, even simple animals are uncannily good at heading for home ground. During the 1940s, the Dutch biologist Nikolaas Tinbergen – a pioneer of behavioural science – carried out some ingenious experiments to see how digger wasps find their nests. Unlike social wasps, digger wasps breed on their own. The females excavate nest holes in loose earth and sand, each female digging up to six holes, which she stocks with food before laying her eggs. Somehow, the wasp has to remember the position of each hole when she returns with food.

To find out how she does this, Tinbergen surrounded a single hole with a circle of pine cones. He left the cones in position long enough for the wasp to become familiar with them as she came and went. Some time later, he moved the cones a short distance away and waited to see what would happen when the wasp returned. This time, the wasp completely ignored her nest hole and went straight to the centre of the circle. Tinbergen then took the experiment a step further by changing the 'landmarks' and the shape in which he arranged them. He put a triangle (rather than a circle) of cones around the nest hole and a circle of stones further away. Which would the wasp

A sense of place is found throughout the animal kingdom. Insects and birds depend on it when they shuttle back and forth to feed their young, and all kinds of animals, from aardvarks to sea urchins, use it when they head home after collecting food.

go for? In the event, when she came back, she ignored the cones and headed for the centre of the circle of stones. Here, she moved about in an restless way and tried to uncover her 'lost' nest hole by digging up the sand.

This classic piece of outdoor research showed that digger wasps pinpoint their nests by learning the position of prominent landmarks. It also showed something else: for digger wasps, overall shapes are much more important than fine details, which is why they remember circles, rather than pine cones or stones.

The homing instinct

A sense of place is found throughout the animal kingdom. Insects and birds depend on it when they shuttle back and forth to feed their young, and all kinds of animals, from aardvarks to sea urchins, use it when they head home after collecting food for themselves.

The simplest way of getting home is to retrace your steps. But many foraging animals, such as desert ants, wander about as they look for food. For them, retracing their steps would waste a lot of energy, so instead they set off home in a direct line. It

sounds straightforward, but how do they do it when they cannot see their destination? The answer is that animals' homing instinct works by building up a memory map, stored in their brains. Using this, they know when they are nearing home and, just as importantly, when they are drifting off course.

In the case of desert ants, they constantly update their memory maps as they search for food. When an ant has collected all the food it can carry, it sets its course by checking its updated memory map and relating it to the position of the Sun. Other creatures with similar homing instincts include honeybees, which also use the Sun as a compass, making allowance for the fact that it moves across the sky.

The homing instinct can be important at close quarters, too, where it may save an animal's life. Burrowing mammals, such as prairie dogs and meerkats, live in open habitats, which have very few places to hide. They are constantly on watch and, thanks to their memory maps, they can disappear down the nearest burrow the moment danger appears. Things are very different if they find themselves at risk on foreign ground without any local knowledge. In this situation, they have to work out where to go – something that wastes precious seconds in the race to survive.

MEERKATS ON GUARD To escape predators, meerkats rely on keen eyesight and an intimate knowledge of their surroundings. They check carefully for danger before heading off on the hunt.

FEELS FAMILIAR

WE USUALLY RECOGNISE FAMILIAR PLACES BY SIGHT, BUT SOMETIMES A SMELL CAN CONJURE UP FEELINGS OF BEING SOMEWHERE WE KNOW. This fleeting experience is a hint of the instinctive way animals remember home ground. Like us, animals have five 'everyday' senses: vision, hearing, smell, taste and touch. They also have extra senses that we completely lack – such as the ability to detect variations in the pull of gravity or of the Earth's magnetic field. All these senses help them to build up maps of their surroundings, so that they can find their way back to base.

The view ahead

For flying insects, vision is the most important way of recognising home ground. Hoverflies, for example, have particularly good eyesight, which they use as they speed over clumps of flowers in gardens or backyards, looking for the pollen on which they feed. The males memorise the position of the best clumps and do their best to keep rivals away. Dragonflies have even keener eyesight. A dragonfly's hunting territory can be over 250 m across, and within these boundaries, it remembers every major landmark, including individual twigs that make good perches – the ideal place to watch out for other insects flying by.

Birds have even better memories than dragonflies and use them to recognise home ground. Experiments with young flycatchers have shown that within as little as ten days they can remember every tiny detail of the landscape around their nests, a process called 'imprinting'. Birds are also amazingly good at flying home over terrain they have never seen before. A Manx shearwater was once carried by plane from Wales to Boston, a distance of over 5000 km. It found its way back to its nesting burrow in an incredible 12½ days, beating the air-mail letter that was sent to Britain with details of its release.

These amazing achievements do not necessarily mean that birds understand what they see. In one famous case, a blackbird built its nest in an open-sided bicycle shed that was over 100 m long. But the bird became muddled by the shed's design, which consisted of many identical sections. As a result, it started 14 nests in a row. Because its behaviour was driven entirely by instinct, it was unable to stand back, look at the problem and realise its mistake.

Scent leads the way

To a dog, home is not so much a familiar visual scene as a familiar set of smells. Like many mammals, dogs and foxes have a much better sense of smell than we do, along with an extremely good 'olfactory memory' for smells they have encountered in the past. As all pet owners know, dogs instinctively stake out their home ground by leaving droplets of urine on trees and other landmarks. This is called 'scent-marking', and all wild carnivores – from skunks and otters to cats and bears – do it, although in different ways. It is not simply a signal to other animals: it also helps the animal leaving the scent-marks to know where it is. If a dog or cat is moved into new surroundings, its scent-marking instinct goes into overdrive, helping it to get used to its new surroundings and feel at home.

SEARCHING GAZE Outsized eyes and colour vision enable a hoverfly (left) to build up a detailed 'memory map' of its surroundings.

STAKING A CLAIM Rearing up on its hindlegs, a leopard rubs a bush with scent (right). Domestic cats are behaving in a similar way when they rub themselves against tablelegs and chairs.

In oceans and rivers, there is no real difference between smell and taste, because all scents are dissolved in water. Fish imprint on the taste of water in the same way that birds imprint on landscapes or features such as trees. When fish migrate upriver to breed, they literally taste their way back to the place where they hatched. Fish that stay in one place have longer to become familiar with their surroundings, and their mental map can be incredibly precise. The frillfin goby, a small fish from the western Atlantic, memorises its surroundings by swimming over the rocks at high tide. At low tide, it is often cut off in rock pools, but that does not stop it moving around. Using its mental map, it jumps from pool to pool – even though it cannot see where it is heading before it takes a leap.

Sounds like home

When bats hunt, they use beams of high-pitched sound to pinpoint insects fluttering through the air. Finding their way home after a hunt is just as important but calls for quite different skills. A bat has to be able to interpret echoes from all kinds of different objects and use them to decide where it is. Then, once it has done that, it has to fly in the right direction and identify its own 'front door'. For many bats this is the mouth of a cave, which is usually hard to miss, but for the smallest species, such as pipistrelles, it can be no more than a tiny crack in wooden panelling, no wider than a fingertip. The bat's radar picks this up from several metres away, allowing the bat to land beside it and nimbly scuttle inside.

FEELING FOR FOOD The American starnose mole has a ring of tentacles around each nostril. The tentacles are very sensitive to touch, and the mole uses them like fingers to find food. The clawlike paws are for digging.

In South America, the fruit-eating oilbird also uses sound to find its way home. It nests deep in caves, and its echolocation calls are low enough to be audible to human ears, sounding like a series of very fast clicks. Oilbirds also have noisy, piercing calls; yet despite the deafening shrieks of other birds flying alongside it, each bird is able to pick up the echoes from its own clicks.

Feels like home

For animals that live underground, home is somewhere that literally feels familiar. Moles have a superb sense of smell, which they use when they mark their territories, but they also use their sense of touch to remember every twist and turn of their tunnel system – even though it can be many metres long. Neighbouring territories sometimes overlap, but moles have a strong sense of home-ownership, staying in their own tunnels and keeping themselves to themselves.

Most wood-boring animals share this avoidance instinct, which helps them to make the most of their food. But there are some bizarre exceptions: in the sea, sharp-shelled molluscs called shipworms drill their way through breakwaters, ship's hulls and anything else made of wood. If their paths cross, they sometimes carry on, one shipworm slowly boring its way through the other.

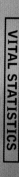

CLASS: Mammalia
ORDER: Chiroptera
SPECIES: *Pteropus*
HABITAT: Tropical forests, grasslands, farmland
DISTRIBUTION: Madagascar, across southern and South-east Asia to China and Australia, and islands in the western Pacific
KEY FEATURES: The world's largest bats, named for their foxlike faces

THE WORLD'S LARGEST BATS

ARE CALLED FLYING FOXES. WITH A WINGSPAN OF UP TO 1.7 M, THEY ARE ALSO THE BATS THAT FLY FARTHEST EACH NIGHT. Flying foxes roost together in hundreds or even thousands, hanging from treetops in colonies known as 'camps'. As night falls, they set off, searching for ripe fruit. Unlike insect-eating bats, flying foxes have large eyes and probably navigate by using landmarks and the Moon and stars.

In the tropics, fruit is in season all the year round, but trees with fruit may be far apart, which is why the bats often have to fly a long way. The outward leg of their journey can be up to 25 km, with several stops en route, before they finally arrive at a tree they may have visited for several previous nights.

They feed by squeezing the fruit and sucking up its juice, discarding the pulp and seeds, which fall to the ground with a sound like heavy rain. About an hour before sunrise, the bats stop feeding and head home.

There are over 50 species of these giant bats, found throughout southern and South-east Asia and some remote islands, such as the Seychelles.

FLYING

FOX

NATURE'S POWERS

AIRBORNE REFUELLING Hovering in front of a flower, a hummingbird sips a meal of nectar. It will revisit the same flowers later in the day, as part of its daily round.

THE DAILY ROUND

MANY ANIMALS ARE DAILY COMMUTERS, MAKING ROUTINE JOURNEYS EVERY DAY TO FIND FOOD. These animals may not travel far, but they have a strict timetable and a strong homing instinct that gets them back to base.

For hummingbirds, the daily round is a fine balancing act between collecting energy and using it up. These tiny birds feed on nectar, and they often follow a set path through their territory, stopping at the same plants in the same order every time. This allows flowers to recharge their nectar before the hummingbird feeds from it again. The plants also benefit, because hummingbirds pollinate their flowers. By topping up their nectar, the plants make sure that their feathered visitors pay them a daily call.

Hummingbirds need lots of energy to fly. They actually spend about three-quarters of their time perching quietly, instead of hovering in front of flowers. These breaks are necessary because a hummingbird's 'nectar tank', its crop, quickly fills up. When this happens, the hummingbird has to wait several minutes until the crop empties, before it can start feeding again. Nectar contains a lot of water, and hummingbirds have to get rid of the surplus in order to be able to fly. If they were scaled up to human size, they would have to jettison an astounding 75 litres a day.

Passing on directions

In Africa's Kalahari Desert, male sandgrouse have the opposite problem: they need to collect water for their chicks. At dawn, thousands of male birds fly off to waterholes up to 80 km away. When they arrive, each bird wades chest-deep into the water, and then squats down so that its chest feathers are fully immersed. These feathers soak up water like a sponge, and when the bird returns to its nest, the chicks squeeze the feathers with their beaks to get a life-saving drink. This daily airlift is the chicks' sole source of water until they are able to fly – a period that lasts up to seven weeks.

Male sandgrouse have an instinct to collect water, but they have to learn where to get it. Younger birds follow older ones, so the knowledge about waterholes is passed on from generation to generation, sometimes for hundreds of years. This kind of traditional behaviour is not uncommon in birds,

especially when breeding. Mummified remains in Antarctica show that Adélie penguins have been using one nest site for over 800 years, returning to it every day during the breeding season with food for their young.

Small-scale wanderers

On rocky shores all over the world, limpets use a mixture of instinct and learning to carry out their daily round. They graze on algae from the surface of rocks, but as the tide falls, they have to make their way back home. For a limpet, home is an oval scar worn away in the rock. Once it is in position, the limpet clamps its shell against the rock, fitting snugly without any gaps, making it

FAVOURED LOCATION Faint oval scars above these limpets show where previous generations have made their homes.

very hard to dislodge. During its travels, a limpet can wander over a metre from its home, but it always manages to find its way back. It does this by leaving a mucus trail and by building up a memory map, which works mainly by touch. As a limpet feeds, it instinctively memorises dips and bumps on the rocks around its home, so that it knows which way to head when the tide starts to turn. If it is moved several metres away to uncharted territory, it gets hopelessly lost.

Instead of returning to a permanent home, many animals instinctively build one when the day's feeding is done. Chimps make themselves platforms of sticks and leaves. Parrotfish spend the night in a slimy 'sleeping bag' made of mucus, which keeps most predators away. At dawn, the fish recycles its bag by eating it and then swims away.

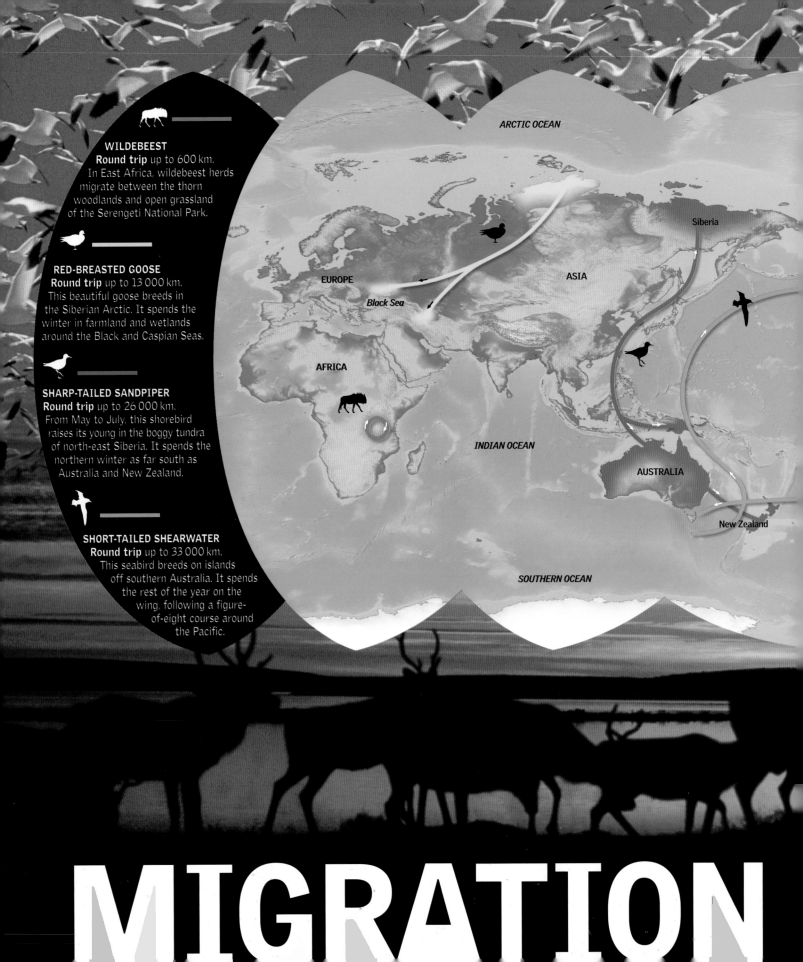

WILDEBEEST
Round trip up to 600 km.
In East Africa, wildebeest herds migrate between the thorn woodlands and open grassland of the Serengeti National Park.

RED-BREASTED GOOSE
Round trip up to 13 000 km.
This beautiful goose breeds in the Siberian Arctic. It spends the winter in farmland and wetlands around the Black and Caspian Seas.

SHARP-TAILED SANDPIPER
Round trip up to 26 000 km.
From May to July, this shorebird raises its young in the boggy tundra of north-east Siberia. It spends the northern winter as far south as Australia and New Zealand.

SHORT-TAILED SHEARWATER
Round trip up to 33 000 km.
This seabird breeds on islands off southern Australia. It spends the rest of the year on the wing, following a figure-of-eight course around the Pacific.

ARCTIC OCEAN

Siberia

EUROPE

ASIA

Black Sea

AFRICA

INDIAN OCEAN

AUSTRALIA

New Zealand

SOUTHERN OCEAN

MIGRATION

GREY WHALE
Round trip up to 20 000 km. Most grey whales feed in the north Pacific, but breed in shallow water off western Mexico.

AMERICAN GOLDEN PLOVER
Round trip up to 17 000 km. This shorebird travels between the North American Arctic and Argentina.

CARIBOU
Round trip up to 1000 km. Caribou spend summer in the tundra and winter in coniferous forests, where food is easier to find.

EUROPEAN EEL
Single trip up to 4000 km. European eels swim to the Sargasso Sea to breed. Larvae drift back.

GREEN TURTLE
Round trip up to 4500 km. One group feeds on the coast of South America, and breeds on Ascension Island.

Map labels: Greenland · Summer · Winter · NORTH AMERICA · Mexico · ATLANTIC OCEAN · EUROPE · Sargasso Sea · AFRICA · PACIFIC OCEAN · SOUTH AMERICA · Ascension Island · Argentina

EVERY YEAR, BILLIONS OF ANIMALS SET OFF ON JOURNEYS THAT CAN TAKE THEM A FEW HUNDRED KILOMETRES, OR HALFWAY AROUND THE GLOBE. Triggered entirely by instinct, migration allows animals to make use of different conditions in different parts of the world. It takes lots of energy, and it exposes animals to all kinds of dangers, including death from exhaustion, drowning or simply getting lost. But thanks to their instinctive navigation systems, enough travellers survive to make the risks worthwhile. The statistics make mind-boggling reading. In North America alone, over 500 million songbirds travel south each autumn and return again each spring. In East Africa, over 2 million wildebeest migrate across the grassland plains. In the oceans, migrants include about 20 000 grey whales and 15 000 humpbacks, as well as untold millions of

turtles and fish. During its 40-year lifetime, a grey whale can migrate over 750 000 km – the same distance as a return journey to the Moon. The Arctic tern has been known to travel from the British Isles to Australia, while the short-tailed shearwater travels around the whole of the Pacific Ocean.

Time to go

Instinct controls almost every aspect of migration. It tells animals when to set off and often takes charge of navigation. At the end of the journey, it tells them when to stop – vital for animals that travel alone and have never seen their destination before. For us, this kind of automatic guidance is impossible to imagine, but it works in a vast range of animals, including insects whose brains weigh just a fraction of a gram.

For wildebeest, migration is often linked to rain, which brings the promise of fresh grass. But for most animals, the trigger for migration is

MASS TRAVEL Instinct overcomes fear as thousands of wildebeest cross a river in East Africa. Every year, some will fall victim to strong currents or to crocodiles.

DEFYING GRAVITY On its upstream migration, a salmon leaps up a waterfall in western Canada. It may take over a dozen attempts to clear a waterfall of this size.

change in day length – the most reliable way of measuring the passing of the seasons. These changes are greatest at high latitudes (those closer to the North or South Poles), which is where most migrants breed. By moving north during the northern summer, they get the benefit of long days and lots of food. In autumn, they travel in the opposite direction, their journey prompted by shorter days and longer nights.

Not all migrants make a return journey. Some short-lived animals, such as moths and butterflies, complete just part of the trip, leaving their young to carry on after they have died. Their migration is like a relay race, involving as many as three generations every year.

Orientation and navigation

Hunters have taken a keen interest in animal migration since prehistoric times. However, scientists have only just begun to unravel the way it works. In many animals, two guidance systems operate hand in hand. One is an orientation instinct, which points them in a particular direction. The other is a navigation instinct, which ensures that they stay on course and complete their journey at the right place.

For migrating salmon, orientation is not difficult once they reach a river mouth. They simply head upstream against the current, leaping any obstacles in their way. For birds, there is no current; instead, instinct tells them which way to go. If wild songbirds are put in captivity, many of them instinctively flutter in a particular direction when the migration season is underway. As the season wears on, they often flutter in a different direction, just as they would if they were steering their way in the wild.

The navigation instinct is more complex. Salmon find their way to river mouths by tasting the water and by using the Sun as a compass. In birds, navigation involves a mixture of clues, including the position of the Sun and stars, and the direction of the Earth's magnetic field. Their navigation system works in all weathers, and it can even operate when a bird can see nothing at all. Proof of this comes from homing pigeons, which head back to their lofts even when fitted with frosted contact lenses – the bird equivalent of a pilot 'flying blind'. However, even a bird's guidance system can let it down. In some parts of the world – such as Kursk in Russia – the Earth's magnetic field is unusually powerful because of large amounts of iron in the ground. When migratory birds are released here, they have great difficulty deciding which way to fly.

MIGRATION DIARY

WORLDS APART White storks often nest on man-made structures during their summer stay in Europe (above left). They spend the winter in Africa (above).

ORNITHOLOGISTS HAVE BEEN TRACKING MIGRATING BIRDS SINCE THE 1890S, WHEN THE FIRST BIRD-RINGING EXPERIMENTS WERE CARRIED OUT IN DENMARK. Today, birds can be precisely tracked using radio transmitters and satellites.

The record migration flight by any ringed bird was set by an Arctic tern in 1966. Between June 26 and December 31, it flew from North Wales, in Britain, to New South Wales, in Australia – a total distance of 18 000 km, assuming it followed coastlines, as terns usually do. Some nomadic seabirds are just as impressive: a sooty albatross ringed in the South Pacific literally flew around the world in 80 days. Unlike terns, albatrosses fly by soaring close to the waves and can stay airborne for weeks at a time. Land birds can also travel immense distances. There are several contenders for the record, one of the most likely being the American golden plover. It shuttles between the Canadian Arctic and Argentina, a round trip of up to 17 000 km.

Inflight corrections

Satellite tracking shows that migrating birds rarely fly in straight lines. They instinctively make inflight corrections to compensate for the wind, and if the wind is gentle these corrections keep them on course. But they can get into trouble in strong winds.

Westerly winds have swept migrating North American songbirds across the Atlantic to northern Europe, leaving local birdwatchers rubbing their eyes. Much larger birds also lose their way. Black-browed albatrosses from the Southern Ocean have been found as far north as Iceland. Once they have crossed the equator, they have little chance of getting back. They need a stiff breeze to stay airborne, and the air over tropical seas is often slack and calm.

For migrating birds, one of the greatest dangers is running out of fuel. Birds instinctively feed up before they set off, and some fuel their voyages entirely with fat put on in the weeks before. This on-board fuel is crucial for land birds making flights over the sea. The ruby-throated hummingbird has one of the toughest itineraries. Weighing just 3 g, this minute bird flies non-stop across the Gulf of Mexico, a distance of over 1000 km.

More birds travel at night than by day, and on clear nights with the wind behind them, millions can be on the move. Many travel on their own or in scattered flocks, but some of the largest migrants – such as cranes and geese – fly in a V-formation called a skein. This has a practical benefit, because each bird creates air turbulence, which helps to pull along the bird behind it. The skein ripples as it flies, and the birds often call noisily to each other as they speed overhead and disappear towards the horizon.

MIGRATION DIARY

This imaginary diary follows the typical progress of a flock of whooper swans on their journey from Russia to the British Isles.

DAY 1 Departure from summer breeding grounds on the marshy shores of the Barents Sea, just north of the Arctic Circle.

DAY 2 After flying past the port of Archangel, the flock of 15 birds arrives at the shores of Lake Ladoga, near St Petersburg.

DAYS 3-4 Bad weather grounds the flock.

DAY 5 The flock scatters after an attack by dogs. After regrouping, they cross the border into Finland, touching down in a lake.

DAYS 6-11 The swans take a break, feeding in fields near the coast.

DAY 12 Fast progress along the southern coast of Finland, helped by a strong easterly wind.

DAY 13 The flock crosses the Gulf of Bothnia, before flying east of Stockholm and touching down for the night. Two birds collide on landing – one breaks a wing.

DAYS 14-15 The injured bird is left behind. The remaining swans lose their bearings in fog.

DAY 16 The flock backtracks to Finland, then turns south to Estonia.

DAYS 17-18 The flock reaches Kaliningrad, where they roost on a coastal lagoon.

DAYS 19-27 Feeding conditions are good, so the swans take another break.

DAYS 28-32 Calm skies allow an uneventful passage across Poland and Germany.

DAY 33 The flock reaches the Waddenzee, in Holland. As they come in to land, one of the birds is killed when it collides with a car.

DAY 35-37 Fog strikes again. The flock remains on the Waddenzee, waiting for it to clear.

DAY 38 After crossing the North Sea, the flock reaches journey's end in coastal marshland in eastern England.

WINTER GATHERING Whooper swans overwintering on Lake Kussharo in Japan's northern island of Hokkaido. The swans, which breed in the far north of Europe and Russia, move south to take up their winter quarters, which stretch from Japan to the British Isles.

OCEAN TRAVELLERS

SWIMMING AT UP TO 80 KM/H, BLUEFIN TUNA ARE SOME OF THE FASTEST MIGRANTS IN THE SEAS. Like turtles, whales and many other migrating fish, they navigate by instinct, travelling enormous distances between their breeding grounds and the places where they feed. Tuna are found in all the world's oceans, and they are always on the move. One fish, tagged off Mexico in 1958, was found five years later off Japan, a distance of nearly 10 000 km. During this time, the fish may actually have travelled some ten times this distance as it wandered in search of prey.

Unlike these nomads, many marine animals show an incredible ability to home in on particular places. Green turtles breed throughout the tropics, returning to the beaches where they themselves hatched. Some breeding sites are not only remote but also tiny: Ascension Island in the mid-Atlantic is only 8 km

THE ONWARD URGE Instinct keeps bluefin tuna on the move, following a network of migration routes in every ocean outside the polar regions.

across and over 2200 km from the nearest land. Yet thousands of turtles find their way there each year. Tagging experiments show that the adult turtles feed along the coast of South America, but no one knows how or where the young turtles travel, because very few are found in the open sea.

A similar mystery once surrounded the European eel, which spends its adult life in rivers and lakes. After as much as 30 years, the eels change colour from green to silver, then head downriver and out to sea. In the 1930s, Danish biologist Johannes Schmidt pieced together what happens next. He discovered that European eels spawn in the Sargasso Sea in the western Atlantic, from where their tiny leaflike larvae make their way back to Europe – a journey that can take three years. Once they reach the coast, they change into adult eels and make their way upstream to feed.

Giants on the move

Many whales migrate to breed. The world's biggest migrant – the blue whale – gorges itself in the icy waters near the poles, before heading towards the equator to breed. At its breeding grounds, its lives mainly on its store of body fat, which can weigh 50 tonnes. Once a female has given birth and her calf is growing fast, her instincts tell her that it is time to move. The two leave the tropics for colder water that teems with food, and the yearly cycle begins all over again.

VITAL STATISTICS

CLASS: Aves
ORDER: Charadriiformes
SPECIES: *Sterna paradisaea*
HABITAT: Coasts and seas
DISTRIBUTION:
   Circumpolar
KEY FEATURES: Record-breaking migrant, travelling between the Arctic and Antarctic.

THE GREATEST MIGRANT

IN THE WORLD IS THE ARCTIC TERN. EVERY YEAR, IT MAKES A RETURN JOURNEY OF UP TO 36 000 KM BETWEEN THE ARCTIC AND THE ANTARCTIC. No other creature sees as much daylight as the Arctic tern, and few other migrants can make such a long journey look so effortless. With its graceful buoyant flight, it can travel such enormous distances because it feeds as it flies. Mostly it stays close to the shore, scanning the shallows for fish. The moment it spots food, it hovers for a few seconds, splashes down to make a catch and then moves on. Arctic terns breed throughout the far north, laying their eggs on bare shingle and sand. Once the chicks have fledged, the terns fly south on one of two routes: down the west coast of the Americas, or along the west coasts of Europe and Africa. When they reach the Southern Ocean, they disperse around Antarctica, before the days start to shorten, triggering their long flight north.

ARCTIC TERN

NATURE'S POWERS

INDEX

A

aardvarks 140, 141
abalones 110
adrenaline 20
Africa 8, 12, 15, 30, 31, 43, 52, 87,
    89, 92, 94, 95, 100, 101, 104,
    106, 109, 111, 113, 147, 148,
    149, 152, 155
Ailuropoda melanoleuca 105
Alaska 48
albatrosses 56
    black-browed 152
    Hawaiian 74
    sooty 152
algae 147
Algeria 3
alkaloids 108
alpha females 119
alpha males 118, 119
Amazon 107
American Sign Language (ASL)
    137
amphibians 53, 63, 73
anhingas 125
Antarctic 76, 77, 139, 147, 155
antbirds 94
antelopes 45, 85, 92, 98, 104, 130
antibiotics 108
antlers 66–67
ants 85, 108, 110, 116, 117, 130,
    141
    army 24, 94
    desert 139, 141
    leafcutter 116
    medicinal 108
apes *see* primates
aphids 28
Aptenodytes forsteri 77
Arctic 43, 44, 81, 139, 148, 149,
    152, 155
Arctic Circle 48
Arctic Ocean 135, 148
Argentina 149, 152
armadillos, three-banded 99
armour, body 99
Ascension Island 149, 154
Asia 14, 47, 109, 118, 148
    South-east Asia 42, 73, 129, 145
Atlantic Ocean 58, 144, 149, 152,
    154
Australia 20, 56, 57, 59, 73, 99,
    101, 102, 145, 148, 150, 152
Aves 57, 77, 155

B

babblers, grey-crowned 28
baboons 84, 120, 121
badgers 28, 45
Bahamas 68
bamboo forests 105
barnacles 46, 60

bats 34–35, 41, 44, 81
    bent-wing 14
    flying foxes 145
    freetail 35
    fringe-lipped 96
    insect-eating 134, 144
    pipistrelle 144
beaches 72, 154
bears 84, 142
    koala 102
    polar 27, 45, 95, 97
beavers 8, 17, 22, 25
bedbugs 68
beekeeping 24
bees 85, 129, 130
    bumblebees 43, 97
    honeybees 8, 24, 27, 85, 87, 129,
        130, 141
    'waggle dances' by 129
beetles
    burying 101
    diving 28
    dung 11, 101
    Namib darkling 43, 44
    stag 37, 66
biological clocks 35, 36, 37, 38–39,
    44
birds 8, 10, 15, 19, 20, 26, 28, 30,
    35, 36, 56, 59, 62, 63, 67, 68,
    69, 73, 74, 78, 79, 82, 83, 85,
    87, 99, 104, 106, 108, 123,
    124, 125, 132, 140, 141, 142,
    144, 151
    flocks of 24
    ground-nesting 74, 97
    male-only brooders 76
    migratory 14, 49
    of paradise 56
    of prey 27, 79
    seabirds 40, 44, 73, 83, 85, 135
    songbirds 42, 45, 49, 74, 97, 149,
        151, 152
    wading 12, 46, 87
    waterbirds 49, 87, 99
    see also individual species
bison 104, 119
bivouacs 94
Black Sea 148
blackbirds 42, 142
boar, wild 85
body language 132–133
body mass 41
bonobos 121, 136–137
boobies 79
    blue-footed 56
Borneo 111
bowerbirds 56, 57, 65
    satin 57
bowers 56, 57
brains 17, 20, 31, 38, 40, 82, 98,
    99, 128, 129, 141
breathing 40
breeding 9, 10, 77, 94, 155
    breeding behaviour 49
    breeding cycles 14, 49
    breeding seasons 61, 95, 147
    see also mating

Britain 152
British Isles 150, 153
buffalo 60, 61
bugs 73, 85
    bedbugs 68
    freshwater 76
    giant water 13–14, 76
    sap-sucking 102, 103
bushcrickets 78
bustards 87
butterflies 38, 43, 68, 78, 97, 102,
    103, 106, 151
    cabbage white 102
    large blue 116, 117
    monarch 38–39, 97, 138–139
    orange-tip 78
buzzards 63, 79

C

cainism 79
California 139
calves 11, 71, 81, 83, 108, 154
camouflage 91, 99
Canada 48, 49, 139, 150, 152
cannibalism 78–79
cardinals, American 83
caribou 149
Carlsbad Caverns 35
Carnivora 105
Caspian Sea 148
cassowaries 76
Castor canadensis 25
caterpillars 22–23, 38, 78, 79, 102,
    103, 116, 117
cats 10, 28, 52, 53, 85, 87, 92, 99,
    108, 123, 132, 142
    wild 132
    see also individual species
cattle 104
caves 35, 42, 60, 81, 106, 108,
    144
Central America 56, 94
Cephalopoda 131
chameleons 132
Charadriiformes 155
cheetahs 30, 92, 95, 98
chemical signals 94, 116, 130
    see also pheromones
chicks 11, 19, 32, 33, 37, 74, 77, 81,
    82, 87, 97, 155
chimpanzees 73, 88–89, 108,
    110–111, 121, 125, 127, 128,
    137, 147
    facial expressions in 132, 133
China 105, 117, 145
Chiroptera 145
chrysalises 38–39, 60
cicadas 59
    periodical 37, 38, 39
clams 110
    giant 53
clans (of dolphins) 135
claws 55, 115, 132
clay, medicinal 106, 107, 108
coasts 46
cockroaches 98

colour, changes of 131, 132
communication 11, 126–137
    body language 132–133
    chemical 94, 130
    sonar 134–135
    through dance 129
    with humans 136–137
conflict
    conflict resolution 120–121
    inner conflict 122–123
copycat behaviour 33, 111
coral 46, 53
    coral reefs 98, 131
cormorants 125
Costa Rica 53, 72
courtship 8, 49, 52–53, 56, 57,
    62–65, 77
    see also mating
crabs 46, 66, 110
    fiddler 46, 55, 56
    ghost 56
    hermit 22, 23–24
cranes 8, 152
    Japanese 51
crickets
    field 20
    mole 58
crocodiles 12, 74, 87, 150
crows 30, 87, 89, 108
    New Caledonian 109
crustaceans 95, 110
    marine 60
cubs 32, 73, 86–87, 89, 119
cuckoos 9, 31, 83
cud, chewing the 104
curlews 87
cuttlefish 132

D

daily rhythms 42–45, 147
dams, beavers' 8, 17, 22, 25
dances
    by bees 129
    mating dances 8, 14, 51, 53, 57,
        62, 63, 64–65
darters 125
dawn chorus 42
days, length of 48
deer 30, 81
    red 53, 66–67
defence of young 11, 84–87
Denmark 152
dickcissels 42
dingos 122
dinosaurs 125
Disney Epcot Center 135
displacement behaviour 113, 123
distraction displays 87
diurnal animals 36–37, 42, 44, 131
dogs 10, 41, 87, 92, 119, 122, 142
    African 73
dolphins 68, 89, 134–135
    Atlantic spotted 68, 134
    Risso's 134–135
    river 134
Dorylus species 94

dragonflies 40, 68, 142
drones (honeybees) 85
droppings 101
ducks 98, 122, 123
  eider 89
  mallard 74

E
eagles 79
  martial 84–85
earth, medicinal 108
earthworms *see* worms
earwigs 85
East Africa 8, 87, 104, 106, 148, 149, 150–151
echolocation 81, 134, 135, 144
Eciton species 94
ecosystem 100
eels 97
  European 149, 154
  moray 128
egg cells 63, 68
eggs
  birds' 8, 11, 19, 20, 21, 31, 49, 56, 73, 74, 77, 79, 83, 87, 110, 111, 155
  crocodiles' 74
  giant clams' 53
  horseshoe crabs' 46
  insects' 11, 14, 23, 62, 68, 78, 85, 94, 97, 101, 102, 116, 140
  smashing of (by vultures) 11, 109, 110, 111
  spiders' 69
  toads' 76
  turtles' 72
electrical signals 40
elephants 10, 11, 15, 40, 41, 68, 73, 84, 89, 106, 108, 113
emus 76
endogenous activities 40
entrainment 39
escape action 98–99
estuaries 46
ethyl mercaptan 100
Europe 14, 33, 42, 47, 76, 109, 117, 118, 148, 149, 152, 153, 154, 155
evolution (of instinct) 10, 124–125
eyesight 18, 25, 27, 45, 53, 63, 81, 92, 98, 99, 100, 114, 134, 141, 142

F
facial expressions (in chimps) 133
falcons, peregrine 89
feeding *see* food
fertilisation 53, 62, 68
filter-feeding 95
finches 42, 59
  woodpecker 109
fireflies 55, 56
  Japanese 54
  pyralis 55

fish 10, 12, 14, 23, 24, 58, 68, 73, 76, 92, 98, 134, 144, 150, 155
  angler fish 68
  cichlids 76, 87
  cleaner 9, 128
  frillfin gobies 144
  frogfish 95
  jawfish 76
  migrating 154
  ocean sunfish 72, 73
  parrotfish 147
  plankton-eating 37
  Siamese fighting 55
  snappers 24
  sticklebacks 123
  tunas, bluefin 154
  see also eels; sharks
flatworms 10
flehmen behaviour 61
flies 8
  dance 62
  fruit 39
  houseflies 98, 124
  hoverflies 142
  yellow dung 101
  see also fireflies
flocks 3, 24
Florida 82, 135
flycatchers 142
flying foxes 145
food 82–83, 90–111
  food-washing 32–33
  hunting for 92–97
    using tools 11, 89, 109–111
  plant-eaters 102–105
  recognition of 96–97
  scavenging for 100–101
  storage of 47, 104
forests 42, 53, 57, 94, 96, 115, 127, 145, 149
formic acid 108
foxes 28, 32, 87, 89, 96, 142
  red 73
frogs 14, 58, 94, 96, 99, 125
  bullfrogs 96
  common 72
  red-eyed treefrogs 59

G
Galápagos Islands 99, 109
gallinules 87
gamebirds 27, 67, 73, 74
gannets 40, 65, 125, 132
  colonies of 81
Gardner, Allen and Beatrice 137
gazelles 81, 92
  Thomson's 130
geckos, house 33
geese 20–21, 80, 85, 98, 152
  Canada 20–21
  red-breasted 148
genes 20, 21, 32, 51, 63, 66, 73, 85, 124, 125
geophagy 106
gibbons 42
giraffes 13, 63

gizzards 106
glucose 20
glycosides 97
goosanders 123
gorillas 111, 137
goslings 80
grass, medicinal 108
grasshoppers 58, 60, 102
grassland 101, 104, 106, 115, 117, 145, 148, 149
gravity, pull of 142
grebes 63, 64–65, 87
  courtship rituals of 64–65
  great crested 64
  western 65
grooming 43, 121, 123, 124, 125
grouse
  ruffed 81
  sage 67
  sandgrouse 11, 147
growth (of young) 88–89
grubs 23, 37, 97, 101, 110, 116, 117, 130
guinea pigs 41
Gulf of Mexico 152
gulls 24, 44, 85, 97, 99, 110, 132
  herring 82

H
habituation 30
hamsters 104
hares 83, 98
hearing 28, 142
  see also sound
heart rates 40–41
hedgehogs 28, 29
herds 11, 15, 40, 73, 84, 104, 108, 113
herons 97
  black 12
hibernation 41, 47, 49, 63, 117
hives 24, 129, 130
Hokkaido 153
homing instincts 140–147
honeycombs 129
hormones 20, 38, 82
horns, crossing of 114
horses 41, 60, 83, 124, 125
horseshoe crabs 46
hoverflies 142
hummingbirds 40, 146, 147
  ruby-throated 152
hunger 43, 91
hunting 14, 32, 33, 37, 40, 43, 89, 91, 92–97, 99, 131, 142, 144
  pack hunters 14, 92, 94
  sit-and-wait hunters 12, 95
  solitary hunters 14
hyenas 14
Hymenoptera 94

I
Iceland 152
Imo (the macaque) 32–33
imprinting 80–81, 142, 144

inbuilt rhythms (of life) 40–41
incubation 73, 74, 77, 125
Indian Ocean 131, 148
Indonesia 45, 56
Insecta 94, 117
insects 14, 28, 33, 36, 37, 40, 43, 53, 55, 62, 68, 69, 78, 94, 97, 99, 102, 108, 110, 139, 140, 141, 142
  leaf-cutting 116
  parasitic 97
  plant-eating 102, 103
  social 85, 87, 94, 116, 130, 140
  see also individual species
instinct 8–15, 16–33, 124–125
iodine 108
isoamyl acetate 27

J
jacanas 65
  northern 67
Jacobson's organ 60, 61
jaguars 99
Japan 33, 51, 117, 153, 154
jays 104, 108
  blue 97
jellyfish 20
joeys 75, 76
juvenile hormone 38

K
Kalahari Desert 147
kangaroos 73, 75, 122
  red 74
Kanzi (the bonobo) 136–137
kaolin 108
katydids 102
Kenya 15
killing of young 73
kittens 28, 87, 89, 132
kiwis 76
koalas 102
Komodo dragons 78, 79
kookaburras 85
Koshima Island (Japan) 33
krill 95
Kursk (Russia) 151

L
Lake Kussharo 153
Lake Wollumboola 48–49
lammergeiers 101
language 126–137
  body 132–133
  chemical communication 130
  communicating through dance 129
  communicating with humans 136–137
  language research 137
  sonar messages 134–135
lapwings 87
larvae 37, 38, 46, 53, 154
lateral lines 24, 92

leaf-cutting insects 116
leaf-eating insects 102, 103
learned behaviour 9, 10, 11, 14, 28, 30–31, 32–33
leks 67
leopards 14, 52, 53, 106, 108, 142–143
Lepidoptera 117
leverets 83
lice, bird 97
lilytrotters 67
limpets 147
lions 14, 26, 30, 62, 73, 91, 92, 108
lizards 33, 94
   baselisk 98–99
   Jesus Christ 98
   Komodo dragons 78, 79
   savanna monitor 43
lodges, beavers' 25
Lorenz, Konrad 21, 80
lunar rhythms (of life) 42, 46

M

macaques
   Barbary 120
   Japanese 32, 33
macaws 106, 107
Maculinea arion 117
Madagascar 145
magnetic field, Earth's 142, 151
magpies 27
Mala Mala game reserve 52
Mammalia 25, 47, 105, 145
mammals 36, 40, 49, 62, 63, 68, 69, 73, 74, 81, 82, 83, 84, 87, 97, 98, 108, 123, 124
   carnivorous 99, 108
   grazing 85, 104, 108
   hoofed 60, 61, 63
   sea 68, 82
   see also individual species
manatees 82
mangrove swamps 46, 56
mantises, praying 68, 69, 95, 99
Marmota species 47
marmots 47
marsupials 74, 76, 102
mating 50–53, 54–57, 66–67, 68–69
   of amphibians 53, 63
   of birds 68
   courtship 8, 49, 52–53, 56, 57, 62–65, 77
   death during 62, 68, 69
   of fish 68
   of insects 55, 62, 68, 69
   of mammals 49, 63, 68
   mating balls 63
   mating dances 8, 14, 51, 53, 57, 62, 63, 64–65
   reproduction 51, 52
   of reptiles 63
   of scorpions 14, 62, 63
   of sea mammals 68
   see also breeding

mayflies 37
mediation 121
medicines, natural 106–108
   alkaloids 108
   antibiotics 108
   formic acid 108
   iodine 108
   kaolin 108
   salt 106, 108
   silica 108
   see also self-medication
meerkats 43, 85, 141
megapodes 73
memory 141, 142, 147
   olfactory memory 142
Mexico 139, 149, 154
mice, house 73
midges 40
migration 3, 8, 10, 14, 15, 31, 37, 48, 104, 139, 144, 148–155
   of whooper swans 153
millipede, pill 99
mimicry 59, 91, 99, 135
moles 144
   starnose 144
molluscs 46, 53, 110, 144
Mongolia 104, 124
monitor, savanna 43
monkeys 32, 33, 108, 125
   proboscis 127
   vervet 11
Montana 25, 49, 115
the Moon 29, 46, 53, 145
   lunar rhythms 42, 46
mosquitoes 40
moths 14, 15, 28–29, 33, 60, 102, 103, 151
   cinnabar 60
   emperor 60
   hornet clearwing 99
   vapourer 60
motmots 26, 27
moulting 73
Mount Elgon (Uganda) 106, 108
mouthbrooders 87
muscles 20, 27, 40, 43
   thoracic 98
mussels 33, 46

N

Namib coastal desert 44
navigation 29, 49, 92, 145, 149, 150, 151
nectar 147
nerves 20, 27, 40, 92
nestlings 74, 82–83, 89
nests
   birds' 21, 30–31, 56, 73, 81, 82–83, 87, 142, 147
   building of 30–31
   insects' 8, 22, 23, 85, 87, 116, 140, 141
   sticklebacks' 123
   turtles' 72
New Guinea 56
New Mexico 35

New South Wales 49, 152
New Zealand 148
newts 62
   crested 53
nictitating membranes 25
night rhythms 44
nightjars 44
nocturnal animals 33, 36–37, 39, 44, 55, 60, 101
North America 25, 46, 47, 55, 65, 97, 100, 104, 110, 115, 118, 119, 139, 149, 152
northern flickers 125
Northern Hemisphere 48
nutcrackers 104
   Clarke's 104

O

oceans 42, 58, 144, 149
Octopoda 131
Octopus cyanea 131
octopuses 10, 132
   day 131
oilbirds, fruit-eating 144
opossums, Virginia 73, 76
orang utans 111
orcas 135
orientation 151
ostriches 76
   eggs of 11, 109, 110
otters 89, 142
   sea 110
owls 44, 79
   barn 28, 44, 45
oxygen 40
oxytocin 82
oystercatchers 33
oysters 46

P

Pacific islands 145
Pacific Ocean 58, 92, 131, 149, 150, 152
packs 73, 92, 113, 118–119, 122
pandas, giant 102, 105
paramecium 20
parasites 97, 108, 128
parenting 14, 72–89
   approaches to 72–77
   cannibalism by parents 78–79
   defence of young 84–87
   family ties 80–81
   feeding of young 73, 82–83
   foster parents 31, 83
   growth of young 88–89
   killing of young 73, 78–79
   protective parents 74–77
parrots 59, 106, 109, 125
partridges 74
Passeriformes 57
Patterson, Dr Francine 137
peacocks 56, 65
pelicans, Australian 49
'penguin dances' (by grebes) 64–65

penguins 65
   Adélie 147
   emperor 37, 76, 77
   king 37
Peru 106, 107
petrels, storm 44
phalaropes 65
   red 76
pheromones 27, 60, 63, 94, 116, 130
pigeons 30, 106
   homing 151
plankton 36, 37
plant-eaters 102–105
plants, medicinal 108
play, animals at 89
plovers 87
   American golden 149, 152
pods 135
polar regions 151, 154
pouches 74, 75, 76
prairie dogs 47, 115–116, 141
predators 11, 12, 44, 56, 72, 73, 76, 78, 87, 91, 92, 95, 96, 97, 98, 99, 116, 117, 123, 130, 141, 147
preening 10, 26, 123, 124, 125
prey 98, 99
   recognition of 96–97
   tracking down of 95
primates 32, 44, 88, 110, 111, 120–121, 125, 127, 137
   see also individual species
Pteropus species 145
Ptilonorhynchus violaceus 57
puffins 83
   Atlantic 56
pups 73, 81, 83, 119

Q

QMP (queen mandibular pheremone) 130
quail 74
queens 85, 94, 130
quetzals 56

R

rabbits 41
racoons 97
rats 41, 87
   brown 116
reconciliation 121
reproduction *see* mating
reptiles 43, 63, 74, 108, 124
   armoured 99
   see also individual species
rhinoceroses 66, 68
   black 114
rhythms of life 34–49
   biological clocks 35, 36, 37, 38–39, 44
   daily rhythms 42–45
   inbuilt rhythms 40–41
   lunar rhythms 42, 46
   yearly rhythms 48–49

ritualised behaviour 125
rivers 144, 151
robins 65
    European 26, 27, 42, 55
Rocky Mountains 119, 139
Rodentia 25, 47
rodents 25, 36, 44, 47, 104, 116
    see also individual species
role reversal 76
rushing displays (by grebes) 65
Russia 117, 151, 153
rutting 66, 67

S
salmon 35, 150, 151
    chinook 69
    sockeye 48, 49, 69
salt licks, medicinal 106, 108
sandgrouse 11, 147
sandpipers
    purple 87
    sharp-tailed 148
Sargasso Sea 149, 154
Savage-Rumbaugh, Dr Sue 137
savannah 15, 114
scarabs 101
scavengers 100–101
scent, signalling with 60–61, 115,
    116, 130, 142
Schmidt, Johannes 154
scorpions 14, 62, 85
    African fat-tailed 63
sea anemones 20, 23, 24
sea slugs 10
sea urchins 140, 141
seahorses 76
seals 40, 44, 83
    elephant 53, 66
    fur 92–93
    harp 80–81
seaweed, medicinal 108
seed-collectors 104
seed-eaters 106
self-medication 106–108
    using ants 108
    using clay 106, 107, 108
    using earth 108
    using grass 108
    using plants 108
    using salt licks 106, 108
    using seaweed 108
    see also medicines, natural
semiochemicals 130
senses 142
Serengeti National Park 104, 148
Seychelles 99, 145
sharks 24, 78, 97
    cookiecutter 97
    great white 92–93
    livebearing 79
    sandtiger 79
shearwaters 44
    Manx 142
    short-tailed 148, 150
shellfish 110
shipworms 144

shoals 24, 40
short-sightedness 18, 114
shrews 41, 81, 85, 101
    pygmy 43
shrimps 23
    cleaner 128
    mantis 95
    snapping 59
Siberia 47, 104, 148
Sierra Madre (Mexico) 139
sight *see* eyesight
signalling systems 53, 54, 55, 56,
    114–115
    signalling with scent 60–61
    signalling with sound 58–59,
        134–135
silica 108
silk 18, 62, 97
skeins 152
skill-sharing 32, 33
skuas 44
skunks 142
smell 27, 60, 68, 92, 97, 100, 101,
    102, 114, 115, 116, 117, 130,
    142, 144
snails 110
    marine 60
snakes 26, 27, 60, 73, 94
    adders 73
    coral 97
    gaboon vipers 95
    North American garter 63
    rattlesnakes 55
    sea 97
songs 20, 58, 59
sound 81, 96, 144
    hunting by 45
    signalling with 58–59, 134–135
South Africa 52, 99, 104
South America 94, 96, 108, 144,
    149, 154
Southern Ocean 37, 71, 77, 135,
    148, 152, 155
sparrows 44
spawning 46, 53, 72, 154
    spawning grounds 49
sperm 14, 53, 62, 68
spermatophores 62
Sphenisciformes 77
spiders 9, 19, 53, 55, 62, 69, 73,
    78, 94, 95, 97
    house 55
    orb-weaver 53
    orb-web 18, 19
    Sydney funnel-web 55
    water 22, 23
    web-building 53
spiders' webs 9, 18–19, 23, 53, 97
springboks 104
squid 132
squirrels 36
    flying 36, 39
stalking 91, 92
Stanford University 137
starlings 2–3, 59, 108, 132
Sterna paradisaea 155
stick insects 102

sticks
    as tools 111
    as weapons 110
stoats 87
stomatopods 95
stones
    as tools 11, 89, 101, 109–111
    as weapons 110
storks 132, 152
strength, tests of 66–67
stridulation 58
suckling 82–83, 88
Sumatra 111
the Sun 37, 46, 77, 129, 141, 151
swallows, barn 13–14
swans
    black 48–49
    whooper 153
        migration diary of 153
swarms 8, 94
swifts, common 45, 68

T
tadpoles 23, 76
Tambopata River (Peru) 106
Tanzania 108
tarsiers 44, 45
taste 142, 144
tentacles 144
termites 8, 85, 89, 110
terns 73, 85
    Arctic 139, 150, 152, 155
territories 55, 85, 114, 122, 123,
    144
Texas 115
thoraxes 40
thrashers, brown 59
thrushes 110
ticks 19
tides 37, 46, 147
    spring tides 46
tigers 20, 52, 55, 86–87, 108, 113,
    114, 115
timetables, instinctive 42–49
Tinbergen, Nikolaas 123, 140
tits 42
    blue tits 28
    great 82–83
toads 99
    common 63
    midwife 76
tools, use of 11, 89, 101, 109–111
tortoises, giant 99
touch 18, 27, 94, 142, 144, 147
toxins (in diet) 106, 107
trigger mechanisms 8, 26–27
    for migration 150
    wrong kinds of 28–29, 83
tundra 148, 149
turtles 72, 73, 150, 154
    green 149, 154

U
Uganda 106
USA 25, 37, 48, 49, 100

V
voles 45
von Frisch, Karl 129
vultures 100, 101
    bearded 101
    black 101
    Egyptian 11, 101, 109, 110, 111
    griffon 101
    turkey 100
    white-backed 100

W
'waggle dances' (by bees) 129
Wales 152
warthogs 85
wasps 85, 97, 140
    digger 140, 141
    potter 22–23
water rails 87
waterholes 12–14, 106, 114
weaverbirds 30–31, 56
webs, spiders' 9, 18–19, 23, 53, 97
West Africa 89, 95
wetlands 148
whales 18, 40, 68, 83, 134, 154
    Atlantic humpbacks 58
    beluga 134
    blue 41, 83, 88, 95, 154
    grey 68, 149
    humpback 58, 59, 68, 70–71, 73,
        149
    killer 135
    Pacific humpback 58
    sperm 92
    whaling 92
wild boar 85
wildebeest 8, 12, 80, 81, 88, 104,
    148, 149, 150–151
withdrawal reflex 20
wolves 113, 118–119, 122
    grey 49, 118–119
wood-borers 144
woodlands 42, 148
woodlice 116
woodpeckers 125
    acorn 104
workers (insects) 85, 87, 116, 129,
    130
worms 94
    earthworms 26, 27, 43
    marine 60

Y
yearly rhythms (of life)
    48–49
young animals 71–76, 78–81
    abandonment of 83
    defence of 11, 84–87
    feeding by 97
    feeding of 82–83
    growth of 88–89

Z
zebras 62, 104

PICTURE CREDITS

Abbreviations: T = top; M = middle; B = bottom; L = left; R = right

Front cover: arcticphoto.com/Bryan & Cherry Alexander
Back cover: National Geographic Image Collection/Kim Wolhuter.
1 FLPA/Minden Pictures/Frans Lanting. **2-7** Getty Images /AFP/Fayez Nureldine. **3-6** Background: Digital Illustrator/Jurgen Ziewe; left to right and top to bottom: ardea.com/John Daniels, TL; Hugh Anderson, TR; ardea.com/ Masahiro Iijima, BL; ardea.com/M Watson, M; National Geographic Image Collection/Beverly Joubert, BL; photolibrary.com/Mark Deeble & Victoria Stone, BR; John Lind, T; DRKPHOTO/Stephen G. Maka, B; FLPA/Winfried Wisniewski, T; NHPA/Daniel Heuclin, BL; ardea.com/Yves Bilat, BR. **8-9** naturepl.com/ Eric Baccega. **10-11** FLPA/Minden Pictures/Konrad Wothe, 1; Olivier Grunewald, 2; ardea.com/ Auscape/Mike Osmond, 3; National Geographic Image Collection/Norbert Rosing 4; ardea.com/ Jean-Paul Ferrero, 5; National Geographic Image Collection/Michael Lewis, 6; SeaPics.com/Tim Calver, 7; National Geographic Image Collection/ Paul Nicklen, 8. **12-13** Background: AUSCAPE/Fritz Polking; left to right: SeaPics.com/Doc White, 1; naturepl.com/Michael Durham, 2; naturepl.com /Michael Pitts, 3; naturepl.com /Anup Shah, 4; ardea.com/Jean-Paul Ferrero, 5; FLPA/Minden Pictures/Michael & Patricia Fogden, 6. **14-15** DRKPHOTO/Martin Harvey. **16-17** AUSCAPE/Joe McDonald. **18-19** National Geographic Image Collection/Raymond K. Gehman; artwork: Matthew White, B. **19** National Geographic Image Collection/Darlyne A. Murawski, T. **20-21** National Geographic Image Collection/George Grall. **22** NHPA/Anthony Bannister. **23** NHPA/Yves Lanceau. **24** National Geographic Image Collection/Bill Curtsinger. **25** FLPA/Minden Pictures/Konrad Wothe, **26** FLPA/Peggy Heard, ML. **26-27** photolibrary.com/Bob Elsdale. **28** AUSCAPE/ Wayne Lawler. **29** ardea.com/Elizabeth Bomford, L; ardea.com/Adrian Warren, M; Roy Williams, R. **30** Alamy/Dave Watts, L; C; Alamy/Loetscher Chlaus, R. **31** Alamy/ Loetscher Chlaus, L; DRK PHOTO/Anup Shah, R. **32-33** naturepl.com/Miles Barton. **33** NHPA/Anthony Bannister. **34-35** DRK PHOTO/Stephen J. Krasemann. **36-37** naturepl.com/Bernard Walton. **37** AUSCAPE/ Nature Production. **38-39** naturepl.com/Michael Durham **39** Bradbury & Williams, B. **40-41** NHPA/Stephen Dalton. **41** NHPA/Stephen Dalton, BL; NHPA/Ann & Steve Toon, R. **42** National Geographic Image Collection/ Joel Sartore, B. **42-43** Olivier Grunewald. **43** photolibrary.com/Tim Shepherd, TL. **44** ardea.com/Jack A. Bailey, B. **44-45** FLPA/David Hosking. **45** National Geographic Image Collection/Tim Laman, R. **46** National Geographic Image Collection/Medford Taylor. **47** ardea.com/Rolf Kopfle. **48-49** naturepl.com/Brandon Cole, T; AUSCAPE/Michael van Ewijk, B. **49** National Geographic Image Collection/Norbert Rosing, R. **50-51** naturepl.com/ David Pike. **52-53** National Geographic Image Collection/Kim Wolhuter. **53** National Geographic Image Collection/Darlyne A. Murawski, B. **54-55** photolibrary.com/Satoshi Kuribayashi. **55** National Geographic Image Collection/Michael Nichols, B. **56** naturepl.com/Pete Oxford. **57** naturepl.com/Dave Watts. **58** naturepl.com/ Kim Taylor, T; ardea.com/Auscape/Mike Osmond, B. **59** National Geographic Image Collection/ George Grall. **60** Science Photo Library/Claude Nuridsany & Marie Perennou, L. **60-61** National Geographic Image Collection/John Eastcott & Yva Momatiuk.. **62** Elkhorn Slough Foundation/Greg Hofmann. **63** NHPA/Daniel Heuclin, T; Science Photo Library/Tony Camacho, R. **64** ardea.com/ Duncan Usher, T. **64-65** National Geographic Image Collection/Des & Jen Bartlett. **66-67** ardea.com/Stefan Meyers. **68** AUSCAPE/ Doug Perrine, L. **68-69** naturepl.com/Jose B. Ruiz. **70-71** naturepl.com/Doug Perrine. **72-73** National Geographic Image Collection/Bill Curstinger. **73** NHPA/Mike Lane, T. **74** FLPA/Minden Pictures/Frans Lanting, T; naturepl.com/Anup Shah, B. **75** AUSCAPE/Jean-Paul Ferrero. **76** ardea.com/Ken Lucas, T; National Geographic Image Collection/Tim Laman, B. **77** ardea.com/ Auscape/Graham Robertson. **78** NHPA/Daniel Heuclin, T. **78-79** naturepl.com/Michael Pitts. **79** National Geographic Image Collection/Tim Laman, B. **80** naturepl.com/T. J. Rich, B. **80-81** National Geographic Image Collection/Norbert Rosing. **81** naturepl.com/Simon King, TR. **82** naturepl.com/Todd Pusser, B. **82-83** naturepl.com/ Bengt Lundberg. **84-85** ardea.com/Stefan Meyers. **86** National Geographic Image Collection/Michael Nichols. **87** National Geographic Image Collection/ Beverly Joubert. **88-89** NHPA/Martin Harvey. **89** National Geographic Image Collection/Michael Nichols, B. **90-91** NHPA/Jonathan & Angela Scott. **92-93** SeaPics.com/C. & M. Fallows. **94** National Geographic Image Collection/Tim Laman. **95** photolibrary.com/Frank Schneidermeyer. **96-97** Bat Conservation International /Merlin D. Tuttle. **98-99** NHPA/Stephen Dalton. **99** National Geographic Image Collection/Tim Laman, TR. **100** ardea.com/Stefan Meyers. **101** NHPA/Daniel Heuclin, T; artworks: Matthew White, M. **102-103** National Geographic Image Collection/ George Grall. **104** naturepl.com/Bruce Davidson. **105** ardea.com/Jean-Paul Ferrero. **106-107** ardea.com/Francois Gohier. **108-109** ardea.com/ Jean-Paul Ferrero. **110-111** ardea.com/ Tom & Pat Leeson. **111** ardea.com/Masahiro Iijima, TR. **112-113** National Geographic Image Collection/Beverly Joubert. **114** National Geographic Image Collection/Michael Lewis. **115** National Geographic Image Collection/Dr. Maurice G. Hornocker, T; ardea.com/Tom & Pat Leeson B. **116** FLPA/Minden Pictures/Mark Moffett. **117** naturepl.com/David Tipling T; National Geographic Image Collection/ Darlyne A. Murawski, B. **118** National Geographic Image Collection/Jim & Jamie Dutcher, BL. **118-119** photolibrary.com/Daniel Cox. **120-121** ardea.com/ Jean-Paul Ferrero. **121** naturepl.com/ Karl Ammann, T. **122-123** AUSCAPE/Jean-Paul Ferrero. **123** FLPA/Malcolm Schuyl, T. **124** ardea.com/ Duncan Usher. **125** National Geographic Image Collection/Michael S. Quinton. **126-127** National Geographic Image Collection/Tim Laman. **128** National Geographic Image Collection/Tim Laman. **129** artworks: Matthew White L; Bradbury & Williams, R; AUSCAPE/Anne & Jacques Six, B. **130** ardea.com/Ferrero-Labat. **131** SeaPics.com/David B. Fleetham. **132** NHPA/Ann & Steve Toon. **133** National Geographic Image Collection/Michael Nichols, TL; NHPA/Christophe Ratier, TR; ardea.com/Adrian Warren, BL; National Geographic Image Collection/Hugo Van Lawick, BR. **134-135** SeaPics.com/Tim Calver. **136-137** Great Ape Trust of Iowa. **138-139** NHPA/James Carmichael Jr. **140** National Geographic Image Collection/Tim Laman, L; artworks: Matthew White, R. **141** National Geographic Image Collection/Mattias Klum. **142** FLPA/Francoise Merlet. **143** National Geographic Image Collection/Kim Wolhuter. **144** Science Photo Library/Rod Planck. **145** naturepl.com/Anup Shah. **146-147** FLPA/Minden Pictures/Michael & Patricia Fogden. **147** ardea.com/Ron & Valerie Taylor. **148-149** AUSCAPE/Fritz Polking T; Bradbury & Williams/Geo-Innovations, M; National Geographic Image Collection/Paul Nicklen, B. National Geographic Image Collection/Paul Nicklen, L. **150-151** FLPA/Minden Pictures/ Mitsuaki Iwago. **152** AUSCAPE/Fritz Polking L; AUSCAPE/Ferrero-Labat R. **152-153** AUSCAPE/Jean-Paul Ferrero. **153** Bradbury & Williams, T. **154** SeaPics.com/Doc White. **155** National Geographic Image Collection/ Cary Wolinsky.

NATURE'S MIGHTY POWERS: ANIMAL INSTINCTS was published by The Reader's Digest Association Ltd, London. It was created and produced for Reader's Digest by Toucan Books Ltd, London.

The Reader's Digest Association Ltd,
11 Westferry Circus,
Canary Wharf,
London E14 4HE
www.readersdigest.co.uk

First edition copyright © 2007
Reprinted with amendments 2007

Written by
David Burnie

FOR TOUCAN BOOKS
Editors Helen Douglas-Cooper, Andrew Kerr-Jarrett
Picture researchers Mia Stewart-Wilson, Christine Vincent
Proofreader Marion Dent
Indexer Michael Dent
Design Bradbury and Williams

FOR READER'S DIGEST
Project editor Christine Noble
Art editor Julie Bennett
Pre-press account managers Penny Grose, Sandra Fuller
Product production manager Claudette Bramble
Production controller Katherine Bunn

READER'S DIGEST, GENERAL BOOKS
Editorial director Julian Browne
Art director Anne-Marie Bulat

Colour origination Colour Systems Ltd, London
Printed and bound in China

CONCEPT CODE: UK0138/G/S
BOOK CODE: 636-003 UP0000-2
ISBN: 978-0-276-44194-3
ORACLE CODE: 356500003H.00.24